the
VALIANT

123 DAYS OF
INTERACTIVE DEVOTIONS
FOR MORE THAN CONQUERORS

ROY G. MILLER

R O Y   G .   M I L L E R

the
VALIANT

"Yet in all these things, we are more than conquerors through Him who loved us."
R O M A N S   8 : 3 7

EQUIP PRESS

Colorado Springs

THANKS

To my daughter, Michelle Shearer:

Thanks for spending many hours proof-reading and editing and offering suggestions, but more than that, for urging me to "*Finish it, Dad.*" Your idea that this little book would be a good teaching tool for English as a Second Language teachers, and your confidence that it would be a help to many other people were encouraging words that made me want to *finish it.* Thank you, my dear daughter.

To my granddaughter, Alexa Vujaklija and to my friend, Manuel Polin:

Thanks for being my "guinea pigs" and taking the first several days of devotions to test them out, to see if they made sense. Alexa, as a young mother with a very busy schedule, your plea for me to "*Finish it*" because you needed a concise daily devotional book made me realize that a lot of other busy, young mothers might have the same need. And Manuel, your enthusiastic "*Finish it! Please!*" as well as your offer to translate the book into Spanish were good motivators for me. Thank you, Alexa and Manuel.

To my friend, Matt Lockhart:

Thanks for perusing a sampling of the devotions and giving me editorial advice and suggestions. Your professional comments were very insightful, and the fact that you thought the book to be unique and I should "*finish it,*" urged me on. Thank you, Matt.

INTRODUCTION

VALIANT: The Definition

That powerful, old-fashioned word, evoking mental images of courageous knights and gallant heroes going into battle for their king, is not often used today. That is a shame, for it is a biblical word, and its actual meanings: *"(1) possessing or acting with bravery or boldness: courageou*s; *(2) marked by, exhibiting, or carried out with courage and determination: heroic;"* along with some of its synonyms: *"brave; courageous; stout-hearted; dauntless; gallant; bold"*[1] are descriptions of how Christian men and women should be living victorious lives today. Bold and victorious for and through Christ, their King; bold and victorious for their families, for their friends, and for themselves.

VALIANT: The Challenge

Each day's devotion in this book is concise and can be completed in less than 15 minutes. My challenge to you is three-fold:

1. Commit to 123 days of valiant living. Begin each day by asking the Lord to fill you with His Holy Spirit and to live His life through you that day.
2. Commit to doing the day's devotion each day.
3. Commit to interact with each day's devotion, as follows:
   a. After reading the scripture, ask: "What is it about this

---

1   Merriam-Webster Dictionary. Accessed 15 July 2023. *https://www. merriam-webster,com/dictionary/valiant*

scripture that demands my courage, my boldness, my honor, or my steadfastness?"

b. After you read my thoughts, write your own thoughts in the spaces provided.

c. Record one thing that will enhance your walk with the Lord that day.

d. Record a short prayer.

e. Determine that you will be obedient to God that day.

f. Maintain this powerful word, valiant, as part of your personal character description:

VALIANT: The Reward

Not because of what we do, but because of what Christ did on the cross, we are more than conquerors. And since we are already more than conquerors, let us live each day proclaiming victory, no matter what the circumstances may be, because nothing can separate us from the love of God. That great truth is what should motivate us to be valiant.

SUGGESTIONS FOR THE USE OF THIS BOOK

1. As a personal daily devotional book
2. As one-on-one discipleship activity
3. As a group study for share groups or Bible study groups
4. As an addendum to English as a Second Language studies

DAY 1: Through God

*Through God, we will do valiantly, for it is He
who shall tread down our enemies.*
Psalm 60:12

OBSERVE

Check the trait(s) this scripture invokes:

Courage? _____   Boldness? _____   Honor? _____

Steadfastness? _____   Other? _____

MY THOUGHTS

When worries, troubles, or fears try to invade your life, this Psalm can be your defense by believing it and doing as God directs you to do. Faith and action go hand-in-hand. Also remember that… *God has not given us a spirit of fear, but of power and love and a sound mind (II Timothy 1:7)*. Ask God to tread down your enemies. He will, you know, perhaps even through your valiant actions.

YOUR THOUGHTS

_____

_____

_____

_____

_____

_____

_____

_____

_____

_____

TAKE AWAY

What have you learned or re-thought that will enhance your walk with the Lord today?

_____

_____

_____

PRAY

_____

_____

_____

OBEY

All day. You can do it because He will do it through you if you let him.

DAY 2: The Undivided Heart

Teach me Your way, O Lord, and I shall walk in
Your truth; unite my heart to fear your name.
Psalm 86:11

OBSERVE

Check the trait(s) this scripture invokes:

Courage? _____   Boldness? _____   Honor? _____

Steadfastness? _____   Other? _____

MY THOUGHTS

The undivided heart faces all decisions, disasters, and temptations by going to God in thought, prayer, and scripture, believing God has our well-being in His heart. In contrast, a divided heart seeks God part of the time and the world part of the time, not always listening to and trusting God in the complex, tumultuous and tempting times. The divided heart ends up being a broken heart. Why would anyone want a broken heart?

YOUR THOUGHTS

_____

_____

_____

_____

_____

_____

_____

_____

_____

TAKE AWAY

What have you learned or re-thought that will enhance your walk with the Lord today?

_____

_____

_____

PRAY

_____

_____

_____

OBEY

All day. You can do it because He will do it through you if you let Him.

DAY 3: No Secret Sin

I will walk within my house with a perfect heart.
Psalm 101:2(b)

OBSERVE

Check the trait(s) this scripture invokes:

Courage? _____   Boldness? _____   Honor? _____

Steadfastness? _____   Other? _____

MY THOUGHTS

For you to have a perfect heart, you must not allow "Do as I say, not as I do" to be a part of your life, even when you are alone, and certainly not when you are among non-Christians. Your spiritual and moral walk "within your house" should be a walk with the Lord, just as it should be "outside of your house." No secret sins, not even within your thought life. They cause spiritual palpitations.

YOUR THOUGHTS

_____

_____

_____

_____

_____

_____

_____

_____

_____

TAKE AWAY

What have you learned or re-thought that will enhance your walk with the Lord today?

_____

_____

_____

PRAY

_____

_____

_____

OBEY

All day. You can do it because He will do it through you if you let Him.

DAY 4: Open My Understanding

And He opened their understanding that they
might comprehend the scriptures.
Luke 24:45

OBSERVE

Check the traits this scripture invokes:

Courage? _____   Boldness? _____   Honor? _____

Steadfastness? _____   Other? _____

MY THOUGHTS

When Jesus opened their understanding, the disciples' lives changed, and God used them to change the world. When you want to understand the truth of the scriptures and to grasp the whys of life's upheavals, pray for God to open your understanding, having faith that He will do so. And He will open your comprehension more and more as you keep asking and reading His word. He might even make you a world-changer.

YOUR THOUGHTS

_____

_____

_____

_____

_____

_____

_____

_____

_____

TAKE AWAY

What have you learned or re-thought that will enhance your walk with the Lord today?

_____

_____

_____

PRAY

_____

_____

_____

OBEY

All day. You can do it because He will do it through you if you let Him.

DAY 5: Be Careful What You Pray For - You May Get It.

And He gave them their request, but sent leanness into their soul.
Psalm 106:15

OBSERVE

Check the traits this scripture invokes:

Courage? _____   Boldness? _____   Honor? _____

Steadfastness? _____   Other? _____

MY THOUGHTS

When you really want something and you pray, not seeking God's wisdom, but begging Him to grant your wish, God may indeed let you have that thing. But if "that something" is not in His will, then your soul will suffer. When you pray in God's will, His answer will not only satisfy, but it will also enrich your soul. Are you feasting on soul food or junk food?

YOUR THOUGHTS

_____

_____

_____

_____

_____

_____

_____

_____

_____

TAKE AWAY

What have you learned or re-thought that will enhance your walk with the Lord today?

_____

_____

_____

PRAY

_____

_____

_____

OBEY

All day. You can do it because He will do it through you if you let Him.

DAY 6: Heart Trouble

Do not let your heart envy sinners.
Proverbs 23:17(a)

OBSERVE

Check the traits this scripture invokes:

Courage? _____   Boldness? _____   Honor? _____

Steadfastness? _____   Other? _____

MY THOUGHTS

When you get your focus off God and His blessings, it is easy to look at someone who has everything, who is always having fun, and to think, "If I could just have little bit of that…." Such a thought, if thought often, can become envy. Beware of envy. It is one of the seven deadly sins. God wants you to be successful and happy and joyful – but in His way. Do not envy anyone, not even just a little bit. Envy is bad for your heart.

YOUR THOUGHTS

_____

_____

_____

_____

_____

_____

_____

_____

_____

TAKE AWAY

What have you learned or re-thought that will enhance your
walk with the Lord today?

_____

_____

_____

PRAY

_____

_____

_____

OBEY

All day. You can do it because He will do it through you if you
let Him.

DAY 7: How Are You?

*Direct my steps by Your Word, and let no
iniquity have dominion over me.*
Psalm 119:133

OBSERVE
Check the traits this scripture invokes:

Courage? _____   Boldness? _____   Honor? _____

Steadfastness? _____   Other? _____

MY THOUGHTS
God's Word through the Holy Spirit is the Christian's GPS; that is how He directs your steps. Do not sidestep with the "…but that's just the way I am" excuse for sin. **"**I know I have a hasty temper, but that's just the way I am." "I know I shouldn't have done that, but that's just the way I am." Give Him your "that's just the way I am" sins, and He will change you from "just the way I am" to "not the way I was." Be liberated, not dominated.

YOUR THOUGHTS

_____

_____

_____

_____

_____

_____

_____

_____

_____

TAKE AWAY

What have you learned or re-thought that will enhance your walk with the Lord today?

_____

_____

_____

PRAY

_____

_____

_____

OBEY

All day. You can do it because He will do it through you if you let Him.

DAY 8: Light Up Your Life

Then Jesus spoke to them again, saying,
"I am the Light of the World;
he who follows me shall not walk in darkness
but have the light of life."
John 8:12

OBSERVE

Check the traits this scripture invokes:

Courage? ____   Boldness? ____   Honor? ____

Steadfastness? ____   Other? _____

MY THOUGHTS

To follow Jesus is not just to believe that He is the Son of God, the Savior. All Christians believe that, but all Christians do not follow Jesus. To follow Him is to let the Holy Spirit fill your life, giving you guidance and lighting your way as you make decisions and live your life. The Light of the World lives within you! His light shines when you are obedient to Him, to His word, and to His guidance. Turn on the Light!

YOUR THOUGHTS

_____

_____

_____

_____

_____

_____

_____

_____

_____

TAKE AWAY

What have you learned or re-thought that will enhance your walk with the Lord today?

_____

_____

_____

PRAY

_____

_____

_____

OBEY

All day. You can do it because He will do it through you if you let Him.

DAY 9: Self-Control

Whoever has no rule over his own spirit is like a city broken down, without walls.

Proverbs 25:28

OBSERVE

Check the traits this scripture invokes:

Courage? _____   Boldness? _____   Honor? _____

Steadfastness? _____   Other? _____

MY THOUGHTS

Self-control, a part of the fruit of the Spirit, is a virtue as well as a protection. When you lose self-control, you let your guard down. And just like a city without walls, you may be invaded by an army of destructive forces, including lust, anger, gluttony, and bad behavior. That is why you must rely on the Holy Spirit in every phase of life, causing you to live so naturally in the Spirit that you are automatically protected by the wall of Spirit-controlled self-control.

YOUR THOUGHTS

_____

_____

_____

_____

_____

_____

_____

_____

_____

TAKE AWAY

What have you learned or re-thought that will enhance your walk with the Lord today?

_____

_____

_____

PRAY

_____

_____

_____

OBEY

All day. You can do it because He will do it through you if you let Him.

DAY 10: Fame + Age ≠ Wisdom

*Great men are not always wise, nor do the
aged always understand justice.*
Job 32:9

OBSERVE
Check the traits this scripture invokes:

Courage? _____   Boldness? _____   Honor? _____

Steadfastness? _____   Other? _____

MY THOUGHTS

Neither fame nor age nor great intellect guarantees wisdom. Age guarantees experience, but wisdom comes from God. *Behold, the fear of the Lord, that is wisdom, and to depart from evil is understanding (Job 28:28).* Likewise, long life does not mean a just life. *...The just shall live by faith (Habakkuk 2:4(b); Romans 1:17(b); Galatians 3:11(b)).* Honor the aged and seek their advice, but if their words are not consistent with scripture, they are not wise.

YOUR THOUGHTS

_____

_____

_____

_____

_____

_____

_____

_____

_____

TAKE AWAY

What have you learned or re-thought that will enhance your walk with the Lord today?

_____

_____

_____

PRAY

_____

_____

_____

OBEY

All day. You can do it because He will do it through you if you let Him.

DAY 11: One of a Kind

*For You formed my inward parts; You
covered me in my mother's womb.
I will praise You, for I am fearfully and wonderfully made.
Marvelous are Your works, and that my soul knows very well.*

Psalm 139:13, 14

OBSERVE

Check the traits this scripture invokes:

Courage? _____   Boldness? _____   Honor? _____

Steadfastness? _____   Other? _____

MY THOUGHTS

Be glad of who you are, one of God's marvelous works. God made you exactly the way He wanted you to be, the unique you. Knowing this, are you doing your best to keep yourself the way He wants you to be physically, mentally, and spiritually? You are not your own; you are bought with a price, Christ's blood. He made you, and then He bought you. He has a double hold on you. Does your soul know that very well?

YOUR THOUGHTS

_____

_____

_____

_____

_____

_____

_____

_____

_____

TAKE AWAY

What have you learned or re-thought that will enhance your
walk with the Lord today?

_____

_____

_____

PRAY

_____

_____

_____

OBEY

All day. You can do it because He will do it through you if you
let Him.

DAY 12: Guard Duty

Set a guard, O Lord, over my mouth; Keep
watch over the door of my lips.
Do not incline my heart to any evil thing, to
practice wicked works with men who work iniquity;
And do not let me eat of their delicacies.
Psalm 141:3, 4

OBSERVE

Check the traits this scripture invokes:

Courage? _____   Boldness? _____   Honor? _____

Steadfastness? _____   Other? _____

MY THOUGHTS

Resolve, will-power, and determination are strong and admirable traits, but they, in themselves, are not strong enough to produce godly character. Godly character comes through the Holy Spirit's empowerment of your resolve and will-power and determination to guard your speech, your mind and your action from evil thoughts and wicked works. Candy-coated sin looks delicious, but it is a poisonous delicacy. Beware.

YOUR THOUGHTS

_____

_____

_____

_____

_____

_____

_____

_____

_____

TAKE AWAY

What have you learned or re-thought that will enhance your walk with the Lord today?

_____

_____

_____

PRAY

_____

_____

_____

OBEY

All day. You can do it because He will do it through you if you let Him.

DAY 13: The Overcomer

(Jesus' words): These things I have spoken to you that in Me you may have peace. In the world, you will have tribulation; but be of good cheer, I have overcome the world.

John 16:33

OBSERVE

Check the traits this scripture invokes:

Courage? _____   Boldness? _____   Honor? _____

Steadfastness? _____   Other? _____

MY THOUGHTS

Christ did not promise you a life without problems, but He did promise you peace in the midst of tribulations, challenging you with these words: *Be of good cheer; I have overcome the world.* No matter what trial you might face, you must never give up; you must never lose hope. The faith that saved you is the faith that sets the power of God in motion to get you through tribulation as He overcomes the world. The same faith. Use it.

YOUR THOUGHTS

_____

_____

_____

_____

_____

_____

_____

_____

_____

TAKE AWAY

What have you learned or re-thought that will enhance your walk with the Lord today?

_____

_____

_____

PRAY

_____

_____

_____

OBEY

All day. You can do it because He will do it through you if you let Him.

DAY 14: God's Gifts

Nothing is better for a man than that he should eat and drink, and that his soul should enjoy good in his labor. This, also, I saw was from the hand of God.
Ecclesiastes 2:24

OBSERVE

Check the traits this scripture invokes:

Courage? _____   Boldness? _____   Honor? _____

Steadfastness? _____   Other? _____

MY THOUGHTS

It does not matter if you are wealthy or poor, God has not called you to laziness, gluttony, or drunkenness, but rather to enjoy your work and to be thankful for what He has given you. It is God's intent that you have inner peace and enjoyment in your labor and in your life, if you are living the life and doing the job that He intends for you. Do your best, be your best, and enjoy your best. Your best comes from the hand of God. Nothing is better.

YOUR THOUGHTS

_____

_____

_____

_____

_____

_____

_____

_____

_____

TAKE AWAY

What have you learned or re-thought that will enhance your
walk with the Lord today?

_____

_____

_____

PRAY

_____

_____

_____

OBEY

All day. You can do it because He will do it through you if you
let Him.

DAY 15: That You Might Have Life

But these are written that you might believe that Jesus is the Christ, the Son of God, and that believing, you might have life in His name.
John 20:31

OBSERVE

Check the traits this scripture invokes:

Courage? _____   Boldness? _____   Honor? _____

Steadfastness? _____   Other? _____

MY THOUGHTS

You can know all the Bible stories, and you might even quote scripture, but unless you have faith in Christ as your Savior, then for you, the Bible was written in vain. By believing in faith, you are spiritually born again, you repent, your life changes, and you will have eternal life with Him. Eternity is an extension of now. Believe and enjoy life in His name. Today. And forever. That is why the scriptures were written.

YOUR THOUGHTS

_____

_____

_____

_____

_____

_____

_____

_____

_____

TAKE AWAY

What have you learned or re-thought that will enhance your walk with the Lord today?

_____

_____

_____

PRAY

_____

_____

_____

OBEY

All day. You can do it because He will do it through you if you let Him.

DAY 16: Rivers of Living Water

He who believes in Me, as the scripture has said,
out of his heart will flow rivers of living water.
John 7:38

OBSERVE

Check the traits this scripture invokes:

Courage? _____   Boldness? _____   Honor? _____

Steadfastness? _____   Other? _____

MY THOUGHTS

Just as a riverbed is the channel in which the source water runs, so we, as Christians, are the channels for Jesus, the Living Water, to run out through our lives. If the Living Water is flowing, lives around us will be affected; if it is not flowing, then something in our lives – sin - is damming it. The Source never dries up. The Source is never the problem; the trash in the channel is the problem. Is the Living Water flowing?

YOUR THOUGHTS

_____

_____

_____

_____

_____

_____

_____

_____

_____

TAKE AWAY

What have you learned or re-thought that will enhance your
walk with the Lord today?

_____

_____

_____

PRAY

_____

_____

_____

OBEY

All day. You can do it because He will do it through you if you
let Him.

DAY 17: Simple, Powerful Words

And it shall come to pass
that whoever calls upon the name of the Lord shall be saved.
Acts 2:21

OBSERVE

Check the traits this scripture invokes:

Courage? _____   Boldness? _____   Honor? _____

Steadfastness? _____   Other? _____

MY THOUGHTS

This was the message that Peter preached in his first sermon at Pentecost, quoting the prophet Joel. About 3000 people were saved that day. This message is still true today, and we must proclaim, as Peter did, "*Whosoever shall call upon the name of the Lord shall be saved.*" Simple words. Powerful results. Changed lives. Have you called to the Lord yet? The line of communication is always open.

YOUR THOUGHTS

_____

_____

_____

_____

_____

_____

_____

_____

_____

TAKE AWAY

What have you learned or re-thought that will enhance your
walk with the Lord today?

_____

_____

_____

PRAY

_____

_____

_____

OBEY

All day. You can do it because He will do it through you if you
let Him.

DAY 18: Success

Let us hear the conclusion of the whole matter:
Fear God, and keep His commandments, for this is man's all.
Ecclesiastes 12:13

OBSERVE

Check the traits this scripture invokes:

Courage? _____   Boldness? _____   Honor? _____

Steadfastness? _____   Other? _____

MY THOUGHTS

If having pleasure and having power and having things is your goal, that goal will never be completely satisfied. However, when you love the Lord and obey His commandments, He brings the pleasure or the wealth or the power that He knows will fill your needs and desires. When He gives you goals or dreams, they will be fulfilled, if you obey Him. Conclusion: love God and be obedient; that's all there is to it.

YOUR THOUGHTS

_____

_____

_____

_____

_____

_____

_____

_____

_____

TAKE AWAY

What have you learned or re-thought that will enhance your walk with the Lord today?

_____

_____

_____

PRAY

_____

_____

_____

OBEY

All day. You can do it because He will do it through you if you let Him.

DAY 19: Soul Restoration

He restores my soul.
Psalm 23:3(a)

OBSERVE

Check the traits this scripture invokes:

Courage? _____   Boldness? _____   Honor? _____

Steadfastness? _____   Other? _____

MY THOUGHTS

In times of our greatest need, our saddest sorrow, our deepest doubt – the times when our days seem the darkest and our souls feel worse than weary, the Lord, our Shepherd, can restore our souls. Every day, if we obediently submit to Him, He will keep our souls in good order, so that when the really trying times come, we can go through them, fearing no evil, because *You are with me (Psalm 23:4(c))*. Daily restoration is good for the soul.

YOUR THOUGHTS

_____

_____

_____

_____

_____

_____

_____

_____

_____

TAKE AWAY

What have you learned or re-thought that will enhance your walk with the Lord today?

_____

_____

_____

PRAY

_____

_____

_____

OBEY

All day. You can do it because He will do it through you if you let Him.

DAY 20: The Strength of My Life

The Lord is the strength of my life; of whom shall I be afraid?
Psalm 27:1(b)

OBSERVE

Check the traits this scripture invokes:

Courage? _____   Boldness? _____   Honor? _____

Steadfastness? _____   Other? _____

MY THOUGHTS

We exercise our bodies and eat the proper foods to have physical strength. In the same way, we must exercise and nourish our spirits by Bible reading, scripture memory, prayer, meditation, and obedience to God. We must exercise our faith by believing and acting on the Holy Spirit's guidance and prompting. With the Lord as the strength of my life, what can man do to me?

YOUR THOUGHTS

_____

_____

_____

_____

_____

_____

_____

_____

_____

TAKE AWAY

What have you learned or re-thought that will enhance your walk with the Lord today?

_____

_____

_____

PRAY

_____

_____

_____

OBEY

All day. You can do it because He will do it through you if you let Him.

DAY 21: The Blessed Nation

Blessed is the nation whose God is the Lord.
Psalm 33:12(a)

OBSERVE

Check the traits this scripture invokes:

Courage? _____   Boldness? _____   Honor? _____

Steadfastness? _____   Other? _____

MY THOUGHTS

This principle is true of any nation: *Blessed is the nation whose God is the Lord.* But when a nation rejects the Lord and His teachings, that nation is destined for doom. Our hope lies not in a political party nor in a particular person, but in Jesus Christ. The call now is for individual Christians and God-fearing churches to live godly lives and teach God's truths, all the while praying for God to give us godly leaders.

YOUR THOUGHTS

_____

_____

_____

_____

_____

_____

_____

_____

_____

TAKE AWAY

What have you learned or re-thought that will enhance your walk with the Lord today?

_____

_____

_____

PRAY

_____

_____

_____

OBEY

All day. You can do it because He will do it through you if you let Him.

DAY 22: Why Fret?

Do not fret.
Psalm 37:1(a), 7(b), 8(a)

OBSERVE

Check the trait(s) this scripture invokes:

Courage? _____   Boldness? _____   Honor? _____

Steadfastness? _____   Other? _____

MY THOUGHTS

Three times in verses 1-8 the Psalmist says: *"Do not fret."* To fret is to become irritated or worried or anxious. Fretting does not solve anything. In fact, fretting makes things worse. In the Sermon on the Mount, Christ tells us not to worry, but to *Seek first the kingdom of God (Matthew 6:33a)*. And when we truly seek the Kingdom of God, it is impossible to worry or fret. It's just impossible. Try it and see for yourself.

YOUR THOUGHTS

_____

_____

_____

_____

_____

_____

_____

_____

_____

TAKE AWAY

What have you learned or re-thought that will enhance your walk with the Lord today?

_____

_____

_____

PRAY

_____

_____

_____

OBEY

All day. You can do it because He will do it through you if you let Him.

DAY 23: Hope and Praise

Why are you cast down, O my soul? And
why are you disquieted within me?
Hope in God. For I shall yet praise Him ...
Psalm 42:5(a), 11(a), 43:5(a)

OBSERVE

Check the trait(s) this scripture invokes:

Courage? _____   Boldness? _____   Honor? _____

Steadfastness? _____   Other? _____

MY THOUGHTS

There are times when our souls feel disquiet, not at rest, anxious. The answer comes in the same way every time: hope in God. Don't be cast down, hope in God. It is this thought, this truth, this hope that can – and will – lift our souls out of the dumps and doldrums and into the heights when we truly praise Him. Our hope in God causes us to praise Him, and when we praise Him, He lifts us up and gives us hope. One begets the other.

YOUR THOUGHTS

_____

_____

_____

_____

_____

_____

_____

_____

_____

TAKE AWAY

What have you learned or re-thought that will enhance your walk with the Lord today?

_____

_____

_____

PRAY

_____

_____

_____

OBEY

All day. You can do it because He will do it through you if you let Him.

DAY 24: Words in Action

Whoever offers praise glorifies Me, and to
him who orders his conduct aright,
I will show the salvation of God.
Psalm 50:23

OBSERVE

Check the trait(s) this scripture invokes:

Courage? _____   Boldness? _____   Honor? _____

Steadfastness? _____   Other? _____

MY THOUGHTS

It is interesting that this verse connects praise and glorifying God with having good conduct. No matter how many praise songs you sing nor how many hallelujahs you proclaim, you cannot truly glorify God if you are living a sinful life. If you are not seeing God at work in your life, examine your lifestyle. Behavior matters.

YOUR THOUGHTS

_____

_____

_____

_____

_____

_____

_____

_____

_____

TAKE AWAY

What have you learned or re-thought that will enhance your
walk with the Lord today?

_____

_____

_____

PRAY

_____

_____

_____

OBEY

All day. You can do it because He will do it through you if you
let Him.

DAY 25: The Generous Soul

*The generous soul will be made rich, and he
who waters will also be watered himself.*
Proverbs 11:25

OBSERVE

Check the trait(s) this scripture invokes:

Courage? _____   Boldness? _____   Honor? _____

Steadfastness? _____   Other? _____

MY THOUGHTS

Soul generosity manifests itself in one word: love. Paul expounds
on this in I Corinthians, chapter 13. Jesus simplifies it when
He tells us that the most important commandment is to love
God, and the second most important commandment is to love
others. We cannot truly love without having a generous soul,
and we cannot have a generous soul without loving. One begets
the other. Isn't that rich?

YOUR THOUGHTS

_____

_____

_____

_____

_____

_____

_____

_____

_____

TAKE AWAY

What have you learned or re-thought that will enhance your walk with the Lord today?

_____

_____

_____

PRAY

_____

_____

_____

OBEY

All day. You can do it because He will do it through you if you let Him.

DAY 26: The Power of Words

There is one who speaks like the piercings of a sword,
but the tongue of the wise promotes health.
Proverbs 12:18

OBSERVE

Check the trait(s) this scripture invokes:

Courage? _____   Boldness? _____   Honor? _____

Steadfastness? _____   Other? _____

MY THOUGHTS

Words of scorn and cruelty cut deep into the heart of another, and though forgiveness may later be given, the scar of hurt remains. Through the Holy Spirit, you can speak truth in such a way that your words reflect the power of your convictions, but they are not swords to the other person's soul. Sword-words can kill; wise words can heal, even though they may be hard to swallow.

YOUR THOUGHTS

_____

_____

_____

_____

_____

_____

_____

_____

_____

TAKE AWAY

What have you learned or re-thought that will enhance your walk with the Lord today?

_____

_____

_____

PRAY

_____

_____

_____

OBEY

All day. You can do it because He will do it through you if you let Him.

DAY 27: Just a Closer Walk

He who walks with wise men will be wise,
but the companions of fools will be destroyed.
Proverbs 13:20

OBSERVE

Check the trait(s) this scripture invokes:

Courage? _____   Boldness? _____   Honor? _____

Steadfastness? _____   Other? _____

MY THOUGHTS

If you want to be wise, spend a lot of time with people who live out their faith, knowing that *the fear of the Lord is the beginning of wisdom (Proverbs 9:10).* Also remember that *If any of you lacks wisdom, let him ask of God ....and it will be given to him. But let him ask in faith....(James 1:5,6a).* Wise guys walk with wise guys. That is no joke.

YOUR THOUGHTS

_____

_____

_____

_____

_____

_____

_____

_____

_____

TAKE AWAY

What have you learned or re-thought that will enhance your walk with the Lord today?

_____

_____

_____

PRAY

_____

_____

_____

OBEY

All day. You can do it because He will do it through you if you let Him.

DAY 28: A Higher Standard

But we have renounced the hidden things of shame.
II Corinthians 4:2(a)

OBSERVE

Check the trait(s) this scripture invokes:

Courage? _____   Boldness? _____   Honor? _____

Steadfastness? _____   Other? _____

MY THOUGHTS

We who know the Lord have been called to live by a higher standard than those who do not know the Lord. That higher standard pertains not only to the outward life, but also to our alone times, when only God can see our actions and read our thoughts, the "hidden things of shame." We have a higher calling. A higher standard. No shame. Nothing to hide.

YOUR THOUGHTS

_____

_____

_____

_____

_____

_____

_____

_____

_____

TAKE AWAY

What have you learned or re-thought that will enhance your
walk with the Lord today?

_____

_____

_____

PRAY

_____

_____

_____

OBEY

All day. You can do it because He will do it through you if you
let Him.

DAY 29: Not Forsaken

Do not cast me off in the time of old age. Do not forsake me when my strength fails.... Now also, when I am old and gray-headed, O God, do not forsake me, until I declare Your strength to this generation, Your power to everyone who is to come.
Psalm 71:9, 18

OBSERVE

Check the trait(s) this scripture invokes:

Courage? _____   Boldness? _____   Honor? _____

Steadfastness? _____   Other? _____

MY THOUGHTS

With age, our senses begin to dull and our strength begins to fail, but that does not mean that the Lord is forsaking us. He gives us hope and joy if we exercise our faith as He empowers us to proclaim His strength and His power. He may call us home, but He will not forsake us.

YOUR THOUGHTS

_____

_____

_____

_____

_____

_____

_____

_____

_____

TAKE AWAY

What have you learned or re-thought that will enhance your walk with the Lord today?

_____

_____

_____

PRAY

_____

_____

_____

OBEY

All day. You can do it because He will do it through you if you let Him.

DAY 30: Troops and Walls

For by You, I can run against a troop; by
my God, I can leap over a wall.
Psalm 18:29

OBSERVE

Check the trait(s) this scripture invokes:

Courage? _____   Boldness? _____   Honor? _____

Steadfastness? _____   Other? _____

MY THOUGHTS

Often, the "troops" and "walls" in our lives are mental or emotional or physical problems, which, like invading armies, trap us inside a barrier of hopelessness. But whatever we face, we can be victorious through the power of the Holy Spirit living within us. (Through Christ), *we are more than conquerors (Romans 8:37)*. Battles are not won by cowering. Let God tread down the enemy through you as you Run! Leap! Be valiant!

YOUR THOUGHTS

_____

_____

_____

_____

_____

_____

_____

_____

_____

TAKE AWAY

What have you learned or re-thought that will enhance your walk with the Lord today?

_____

_____

_____

PRAY

_____

_____

_____

OBEY

All day. You can do it because He will do it through you if you let Him.

DAY 31: When the Burden Seems Too Heavy

Cast your burden on the Lord, and He will sustain you;
He shall never permit the righteous to be
moved [to be shaken; to fall].
Psalm 55:22

OBSERVE

Check the trait(s) this scripture invokes:

Courage? _____   Boldness? _____   Honor? _____

Steadfastness? _____   Other? _____

MY THOUGHTS

Sometimes it feels as if personal problems, national turmoil, global conflicts, plus cultural changes are burdens too heavy to carry. But they are not too heavy for the Lord. When you "cast your burden on the Lord," He will strengthen and support you and direct you to do or to go or just to be. Be obedient. Be concerned. But don't be shaken. Let the Lord handle you and your burden as He sees fit.

YOUR THOUGHTS

_____

_____

_____

_____

_____

_____

_____

_____

_____

TAKE AWAY

What have you learned or re-thought that will enhance your walk with the Lord today?

_____

_____

_____

PRAY

_____

_____

_____

OBEY

All day. You can do it because He will do it through you if you let Him.

DAY 32: The Satisfied Soul

A desire accomplished is sweet to the soul,
but it is an abomination to fools to depart from evil.
Proverbs 13:19

OBSERVE

Check the trait(s) this scripture invokes:

Courage? _____   Boldness? _____   Honor? _____

Steadfastness? _____   Other? _____

MY THOUGHTS

If your desire is God-given, don't give it up. God will fulfill it as you pursue it with diligence, and you will have satisfaction deep within your soul. But if you are seeking something that is not in God's will, you may indeed accomplish it, and you may enjoy it as the world enjoys things, but it will not fully satisfy. Your soul will still be hungry, craving something sweet.

YOUR THOUGHTS

_____

_____

_____

_____

_____

_____

_____

_____

_____

TAKE AWAY

What have you learned or re-thought that will enhance your walk with the Lord today?

_____

_____

_____

PRAY

_____

_____

_____

OBEY

All day. You can do it because He will do it through you if you let Him.

DAY 33: Fight Fear. Remember

You shall not be afraid of them,
but you shall remember well what the Lord your
God did to Pharoah and to all Egypt.
Deuteronomy 7:18

OBSERVE

Check the trait(s) this scripture invokes:

Courage? _____   Boldness? _____   Honor? _____

Steadfastness? _____   Other? _____

MY THOUGHTS

When you face fearful circumstances, remember that *God has not given us a spirit of fear, but of power and of love and of a sound mind (II Tim. 1:7)*. Remember that the Lord Himself said, *"I will never leave you nor forsake you." (Heb. 13:5b)* Remember to pray. Remember to read your Bible. Remember how God has helped you in the past. And remember that remembrance is a good fear-chaser. Remember?

YOUR THOUGHTS

_____

_____

_____

_____

_____

_____

_____

_____

_____

TAKE AWAY

What have you learned or re-thought that will enhance your walk with the Lord today?

_____

_____

_____

PRAY

_____

_____

_____

OBEY

All day. You can do it because He will do it through you if you let Him.

DAY 34: Wishy-Washy? NO!

Trust in the Lord with all your heart and
lean not on your own understanding.
In all your ways acknowledge Him, and He shall direct your path.
Proverbs 3:5-6

OBSERVE

Check the trait(s) this scripture invokes:

Courage? _____   Boldness? _____   Honor? _____

Steadfastness? _____   Other? _____

MY THOUGHTS

Hone your thinking skills, sharpen your intellectual prowess, and whet your business acumen; but before you trust in your own judgement, seek the Lord's wisdom. It surpasses yours in every way. His advice may not be what you want to hear, but when He gives direction, go with God. Don't waver, don't be wishy-washy. Trust in the Lord, and do not look back, not even when you do not completely understand.

YOUR THOUGHTS

_____

_____

_____

_____

_____

_____

_____

_____

_____

TAKE AWAY

What have you learned or re-thought that will enhance your walk with the Lord today?

_____

_____

_____

PRAY

_____

_____

_____

OBEY

All day. You can do it because He will do it through you if you let Him.

DAY 35: Strength and Courage

*"Have I not commanded you? Be strong and
of good courage; be not afraid,
nor be dismayed; for the Lord your God
is with you, wherever you go."*

Joshua 1:9

OBSERVE

Check the trait(s) this scripture invokes:

Courage? _____   Boldness? _____   Honor? _____

Steadfastness? _____   Other? _____

MY THOUGHTS

God did not encourage Joshua to "be strong and of good courage." He commanded him to be so. This spiritual principle of strength and courage is still true today. It is a matter of faith. If you believe that the "Lord your God is with you wherever you go," then live like you believe it. Don't fear; don't fret; be strong and very courageous. This is God's command, not His suggestion. (**See Day 54 for further comments.**)

YOUR THOUGHTS

_____

_____

_____

_____

_____

_____

_____

_____

_____

TAKE AWAY

What have you learned or re-thought that will enhance your walk with the Lord today

_____

_____

_____

PRAY

_____

_____

_____

OBEY

All day. You can do it because He will do it through you if you let Him.

DAY 36: What to Do?

There are many plans in a man's heart;
nevertheless, the Lord's counsel – that will stand.
Proverbs 19:21

OBSERVE
Check the trait(s) this scripture invokes:

Courage? _____   Boldness? _____   Honor? _____

Steadfastness? _____   Other? _____

MY THOUGHTS
Should you hope and dream and imagine the impossible? Should you plan and prepare and make to-do lists? Should you use your God-given skills and talents to accomplish your goals? Yes! But only after you have sought God's counsel. Let God give you your hopes and dreams, and then use your God-given skills to make them come true. Man's plans can fail; God's cannot.

YOUR THOUGHTS

_____

_____

_____

_____

_____

_____

_____

_____

_____

TAKE AWAY

What have you learned or re-thought that will enhance your walk with the Lord?

_____

_____

_____

PRAY

_____

_____

_____

OBEY

All day. You can do it because He will do it through you if you let Him.

DAY 37: "As a Man Thinketh..."

You will keep him in perfect peace whose mind is stayed on You, because he trusts in You.

Isaiah 26:3

OBSERVE

Check the trait(s) this scripture invokes:

Courage? _____   Boldness? _____   Honor? _____

Steadfastness? _____   Other? _____

MY THOUGHTS

You cannot have Jesus' peace if you do not think you can. And you cannot NOT have Jesus' peace if you keep your focus on Him and believe His words: *...My peace I give to you, not as the world gives, do I give to you ... (John 14:27).* Perfect peace. What a thought! What a truth! Believe what He says. It is a matter of trust.

YOUR THOUGHTS

_____

_____

_____

_____

_____

_____

_____

_____

_____

TAKE AWAY

What have you learned or re-thought that will enhance your walk with the Lord?

_____

_____

_____

PRAY

_____

_____

_____

OBEY

All day. You can do it because He will do it through you if you let Him.

DAY 38: Loving Jesus

And the King will answer and say to him,
'Assuredly, I say to you, inasmuch as you did it unto one
of the least of these my brethren, you did it unto Me.'
Matthew 25:40

OBSERVE

Check the trait(s) this scripture invokes:

Courage? _____   Boldness? _____   Honor? _____

Steadfastness? _____   Other? _____

MY THOUGHTS

How can you show love for Jesus, whom you cannot see? Feed the hungry, clothe the poor, visit prisoners, give care to widows and orphans and needy persons whom you can clearly see. Jesus says, "*Inasmuch as you did it to one of the least of these my brethren…*". Loving Jesus is simple: Love others. Let the Holy Spirit do His work through your work. Love and care for others, and "*… you did it unto Me.*"

YOUR THOUGHTS

_____

_____

_____

_____

_____

_____

_____

_____

_____

TAKE AWAY

What have you learned or re-thought that will enhance your walk with the Lord today?

_____

_____

_____

PRAY

_____

_____

_____

OBEY

All day. You can do it because He will do it through you if you let Him.

DAY 39: What Goes Around Comes Around

Whoever shuts his ears to the cry of the poor
will also cry himself and not be heard.
Proverbs 21:13

OBSERVE

Check the trait(s) this scripture invokes:

Courage? ____   Boldness? ____   Honor? ____

Steadfastness? ____   Other? _____

MY THOUGHTS

The world is full of poor people, and you cannot solve the world's poverty problems. So, what can you do? Open your ears. Hear the cry of those in need. Ask God what to do. And then, do what He directs, ...*not grudgingly or of necessity, for God loves a cheerful giver (2 Corinthians 9:7)*. You, yourself, might cry out someday. Will anyone hear your cry?

YOUR THOUGHTS

_____

_____

_____

_____

_____

_____

_____

_____

_____

TAKE AWAY.

What have you learned or re-thought that will enhance your walk with the Lord today?

_____

_____

_____

PRAY

_____

_____

_____

OBEY

All day. You can do it because He will do it through you if you let Him.

DAY 40: Don't be a "Gimme-Gus"

The desire of the lazy man kills him, for his hands refuse to labor.
He covets greedily all day long, but the
righteous gives and does not spare.
Proverbs 21:25, 26

OBSERVE

Check the trait(s) this scripture invokes:

Courage? _____   Boldness? _____   Honor? _____

Steadfastness? _____   Other? _____

MY THOUGHTS

Greed. Laziness. Covetousness. These emotions can kill you. Maybe not physically, but they can kill your good will, your self-respect, your relationships, and your internal joy. What is the solution? Get off the couch and do your job the best you can. Be glad when others prosper. And give, give, give: of your money, of your time, and of yourself to God and to others. Let that be your desire. It is a life-giver, not a killer.

YOUR THOUGHTS

_____

_____

_____

_____

_____

_____

_____

_____

_____

TAKE AWAY

What have you learned or re-thought that will enhance your walk with the Lord today?

_____

_____

_____

PRAY

_____

_____

_____

OBEY

All day. You can do it because He will do it through you if you let Him.

DAY 41: Warning

Do not overwork to be rich; because of
your own understanding, cease.
Proverbs 23:4

OBSERVE

Check the trait(s) this scripture invokes:

Courage? _____   Boldness? _____   Honor? _____

Steadfastness? _____   Other? _____

MY THOUGHTS

It is not wrong to be rich. Money is not evil. But as Paul told Timothy: *"...the LOVE of money is a ROOT of all kinds of EVIL, for which some have STRAYED FROM THE FAITH in their GREEDINESS , and pierced themselves through with MANY SORROWS." (I Timothy 6:10)*. Love money? Overworking to be rich? Coveting? Erring from the faith by trusting in riches? Cease, or suffer sorrowful consequences. Understand?

YOUR THOUGHTS

_____

_____

_____

_____

_____

_____

_____

_____

_____

TAKE AWAY

What have you learned or re-thought that will enhance your walk with the Lord today?

_____

_____

_____

PRAY

_____

_____

_____

OBEY

All day. You can do it because He will do it through you if you let Him.

DAY 42: Time for a Spiritual EKG?

So he shepherded them according to the integrity of his heart,
And guided them by the skillfulness of his hands.
Psalm 78:72

OBSERVE
Check the trait(s) this scripture invokes:

Courage? _____ Boldness? _____ Honor? _____

Steadfastness? _____ Other? _____

MY THOUGHTS
King David shepherded his people with the same principle as shepherd-boy David had shepherded his sheep. This principle of having an honest, upright heart and skillful, hard-working hands also applies to pastor-shepherds today, and indeed, to every Christian. Everybody influences somebody, either for good or for evil, "according to the integrity of his heart." How's your heart?

YOUR THOUGHTS

_____

_____

_____

_____

_____

_____

_____

_____

_____

TAKE AWAY

What have you learned or re-thought that will enhance your walk with the Lord today?

_____

_____

_____

PRAY

_____

_____

_____

OBEY

All day. You can do it because He will do it through you if you let Him.

DAY 43: Living Hope vs. Wishful Thinking

Blessed be the God and Father of our Lord Jesus Christ,
who, according to His abundant mercy has begotten us again to a
living hope through the resurrection of Jesus Christ from the dead.

I Peter 1:3

OBSERVE

Check the trait(s) this scripture invokes:

Courage? _____   Boldness? _____   Honor? _____

Steadfastness? _____   Other? _____

MY THOUGHTS

Begotten again = reborn. That is the spiritual birth and spiritual truth for the true believer. That is salvation. Reborn to a living hope, not wishful thinking – a living hope for what God has for us today, tomorrow, and forever all because of Jesus' resurrection. He lived for us, He died for us, and He lives again through the Holy Spirit in every born-again believer. Isn't that amazing? That is Living Hope!

YOUR THOUGHTS

_____

_____

_____

_____

_____

_____

_____

_____

_____

TAKE AWAY

What have you learned or re-thought that will enhance your walk with the Lord today?

_____

_____

_____

PRAY

_____

_____

_____

OBEY

All day. You can do it because He will do it through you if you let Him.

DAY 44: Brawn or Brain? Meekness or Weakness?

A wise man is strong,
Yes, a man of knowledge increases strength.
Proverbs 24:5

OBSERVE

Check the trait(s) this scripture invokes:

Courage? ____   Boldness? ____   Honor? ____

Steadfastness? ____   Other? _____

MY THOUGHTS

It is not wise to be weak, neither physically, mentally, nor spiritually. The greater your strength, the greater is your capability to be meek, not weak. Meekness is the virtue of being strong in the Lord. But, when you are strong in the Lord, you should still be strong in your body, mind, and spirit. Meek, but not weak. That is a strong statement for the wise.

YOUR THOUGHTS

_____

_____

_____

_____

_____

_____

_____

_____

_____

TAKE AWAY

What have you learned or re-thought that will enhance your walk with the Lord today?

_____

_____

_____

PRAY

_____

_____

_____

OBEY

All day. You can do it because He will do it through you if you let Him.

DAY 45: Awaken the Dawn

*I rise before the dawning of the morning and
cry for help; I hope in your Word.*
Psalm 119:147

OBSERVE

Check the trait(s) this scripture invokes:

Courage? _____   Boldness? _____   Honor? _____

Steadfastness? _____   Other? _____

MY THOUGHTS

No matter what your circumstances may be, whether good or
bad, the wise way to start your day is by asking God for His
help: His wisdom, His strength, His guidance. Hope is in His
Word. (And watching the multicolored dawn is an added bonus,
making getting out of bed well worth the effort).

YOUR THOUGHTS

_____

_____

_____

_____

_____

_____

_____

_____

_____

TAKE AWAY

What have you learned or re-thought that will enhance your
walk with the Lord today?

_____

_____

_____

PRAY

_____

_____

_____

OBEY

All day. You can do it because He will do it through you if you
let Him.

DAY 46: Flow, River, Flow

A righteous man who falters before the wicked
is like a murky spring and a polluted well.
Proverbs 25:26

OBSERVE

Check the trait(s) this scripture invokes:

Courage? _____   Boldness? _____   Honor? _____

Steadfastness? _____   Other? _____

MY THOUGHTS

Know what you believe and why you believe it. Know who you are and Whose you are. Every day, live out your righteous faith, not self-righteous words. And when you are with the "culture crowd," remember that Christ, the Living Water, lives within you. Let Him flow out of you and you will never falter. Living Water is never murky.

YOUR THOUGHTS

_____

_____

_____

_____

_____

_____

_____

_____

_____

TAKE AWAY

What have you learned or re-thought that will enhance your
walk with the Lord today?

_____

_____

_____

PRAY

_____

_____

_____

OBEY

All day. You can do it because He will do it through you if you
let Him.

DAY 47: Bold or Brash? Humility or Arrogance?

In the day when I cried out, You answered me,
and made me bold with strength in my soul.
Psalm 138:3

OBSERVE

Check the trait(s) this scripture invokes:

Courage? _____   Boldness? _____   Honor? _____

Steadfastness? _____   Other? _____

MY THOUGHTS

Being bold is not being without fear; it is acting despite fear, doing the right thing, overcoming fear. God makes you bold; fear makes you brash. Or timid. Do not confuse timidity with humility. Boldness overcomes timidity; humility overcomes arrogance.

Could it be that God Himself makes you cry out so He can answer and make you bold?

(See Day 48 for the "strength of my soul" portion of this scripture verse).

YOUR THOUGHTS

_____

_____

_____

_____

_____

_____

_____

_____

_____

TAKE AWAY

What have you learned or re-thought that will enhance your walk with the Lord today?

_____

_____

_____

PRAY

_____

_____

_____

OBEY

All day. You can do it because He will do it through you if you let Him.

DAY 48: Giving and Living

In the day when I cried out, You answered me,
and made me bold with strength in my soul.
Psalm 138:3

OBSERVE

Check the trait(s) this scripture invokes:

Courage? _____   Boldness? _____   Honor? _____

Steadfastness? _____   Other? _____

MY THOUGHTS

Soul food and soul exercise are vital for soul strength. But how do you get soul food and soul exercise? You cry out to God, and He answers by giving you faith, integrity, and boldness (soul food). Then, through faith, you live and act with honesty and high moral principles (soul exercise). His giving and your living out His gifts build your character, which strengthens your soul. Both the giving and living are required for soul strength.

YOUR THOUGHTS

_____

_____

_____

_____

_____

_____

_____

_____

_____

TAKE AWAY

What have you learned or re-thought that will enhance your walk with the Lord today?

_____

_____

_____

PRAY

_____

_____

_____

OBEY

All day. You can do it because He will do it through you if you let Him.

DAY 49: Evening Prayer?

*Cause me to hear Your lovingkindness in
the morning, for in You do I trust.*
Psalm 143:8a

OBSERVE

Check the trait(s) this scripture invokes:

Courage? _____   Boldness? _____   Honor? _____

Steadfastness? _____   Other? _____

MY THOUGHTS

Having trouble getting up in the morning? Hating to face
the day? Worried about what's ahead, or distressed about
what's behind? Memorize this scripture verse and make it your
"Goodnight, God" thought as you "lay me down to sleep." Then
look and listen for God's lovingkindness the next morning. Put
your trust to the test as you put your foot to the floor.

YOUR THOUGHTS

_____

_____

_____

_____

_____

_____

_____

_____

_____

TAKE AWAY

What have you learned or re-thought that will enhance your walk with the Lord today?

_____

_____

_____

PRAY

_____

_____

_____

OBEY

All day. You can do it because He will do it through you if you let Him.

DAY 50: Setting Your Compass

*Cause me to know the way in which I should
walk, for I lift up my soul to You.*
Psalm 143:8b

OBSERVE

Check the trait(s) this scripture invokes:

Courage? _____   Boldness? _____   Honor? _____

Steadfastness? _____   Other? _____

MY THOUGHTS

In the circle of the day, you can go in 360 different directions.
There are too many choices. That is why, each day, first thing in
the morning, you need for God to set your compass, to show you
the way you should walk. Throughout the day, there may be a lot
of twists and turns, so check with Him to make sure you keep on
His course. Lift your soul up to God; He will show you the way.

YOUR THOUGHTS

_____

_____

_____

_____

_____

_____

_____

_____

_____

TAKE AWAY

What have you learned or re-thought that will enhance your
walk with the Lord today?

_____

_____

_____

PRAY

_____

_____

_____

OBEY

All day. You can do it because He will do it through you if you
let Him.

DAY 51: Not Just Words

*One generation shall praise Your works to another
and shall declare Your mighty acts.*

Psalm 145:4

OBSERVE

Check the traits this scripture invokes:

Courage? _____   Boldness? _____   Honor? _____

Steadfastness? _____   Other? _____

MY THOUGHTS

The evidence of your faith lies not only in your words, but in your living and loving it out before your family. What does your family say about your faith? About your life? About your God? As you praise God with your lips, let His Holy Spirit live and love through your life and love, so that your children will praise and declare God's mighty acts to their children...and they to their children....and they to theirs...and...

YOUR THOUGHTS

_____

_____

_____

_____

_____

_____

_____

_____

_____

TAKE AWAY

What have you learned or re-thought that will enhance your walk with the Lord today?

_____

_____

_____

PRAY

_____

_____

_____

OBEY

All day. You can do it because He will do it through you if you let Him.

DAY 52: But What About…?"

*Every word of God is pure; He is a shield to
those who put their trust in Him.*
Proverbs 30:5

OBSERVE
Check the traits this scripture invokes:

Courage? _____   Boldness? _____   Honor? _____

Steadfastness? _____   Other? _____

MY THOUGHTS
Either you believe the word of God, or you do not. There is no
in-between. You do not get to choose which parts you believe
and dismiss other parts as fables or myths. You are not asked to
fully understand, but you are asked to fully believe. And when
you fully believe, when you fully trust Him, He becomes your
shield. Is your shield in place?

YOUR THOUGHTS

_____

_____

_____

_____

_____

_____

_____

_____

_____

TAKE AWAY

What have you learned or re-thought that will enhance your walk with the Lord today?

_____

_____

_____

PRAY

_____

_____

_____

OBEY

All day. You can do it because He will do it through you if you let Him.

DAY 53: God's Got a Secret

The secret things belong to the Lord our God, but those things which are revealed belong to us and to our children forever, that we may do all of the words of this law.

Deuteronomy 29:29

OBSERVE

Check the traits this scripture invokes:

Courage? ____   Boldness? ____   Honor? ____

Steadfastness? ____   Other? _____

MY THOUGHTS

There are plenty of not-so-secret things, things which God has revealed in His word, for you to ponder and to practice and teach to your children. Keep searching, keep learning, keep trying to know the mind of Christ, and some of the mysterious things will seem not-so-mysterious. But the secret things belong to the Lord.

YOUR THOUGHTS

_____

_____

_____

_____

_____

_____

_____

_____

_____

TAKE AWAY

What have you learned or re-thought that will enhance your walk with the Lord today?

_____

_____

_____

PRAY

_____

_____

_____

OBEY

All day. You can do it because He will do it through you if you let Him.

DAY 54: A Command and A Promise

Have I not commanded you? Be strong and of good courage;
do not be afraid nor be dismayed, for the Lord your God
is with you wherever you go.
Joshua 1:9

OBSERVE

Check the traits this scripture invokes:

Courage? _____   Boldness? _____   Honor? _____

Steadfastness? _____   Other? _____

MY THOUGHTS

To the warriors who were to storm and conquer Jericho, God gave a command: be strong and of good courage. He also gave a promise: the Lord your God is with you wherever you go. The principle of these words is true for Christians today. Your Jericho comes in many forms: relationship problems, financial difficulty, spiritual battles, and others. Whatever the problem, believe the promise, and you can fulfill the command.

YOUR THOUGHTS

_____

_____

_____

_____

_____

_____

_____

_____

_____

TAKE AWAY

What have you learned or re-thought that will enhance your walk with the Lord today?

_____

_____

_____

PRAY

_____

_____

_____

OBEY

All day. You can do it because He will do it through you if you let Him.

DAY 55: By Their Fruit, You Will Know Them

Keep your heart with all diligence, for out of it spring the issues of life.
Proverbs 4:23

OBSERVE

Check the traits this scripture invokes:

Courage? ____   Boldness? ____   Honor? ____

Steadfastness? ____   Other? _____

MY THOUGHTS

Your actions, your habits, your motivations, your character—all of the issues of life begin in your heart, or your thought life: bad thoughts produce bad fruit; good thoughts produce good fruit. Guard your thought life, and so keep your heart with all diligence. Produce figs, not thistles.

YOUR THOUGHTS

_____

_____

_____

_____

_____

_____

_____

_____

_____

TAKE AWAY

What have you learned or re-thought that will enhance your walk with the Lord today?

_____

_____

_____

PRAY

_____

_____

_____

OBEY

All day. You can do it because He will do it through you if you let Him.

DAY 56: Even on Monday

Let the words of my mouth and the meditations of my heart be acceptable in Your sight, O Lord, my strength and my Redeemer.
Psalms 19:14

OBSERVE

Check the traits this scripture invokes:

Courage? _____   Boldness? _____   Honor? _____

Steadfastness? _____   Other? _____

MY THOUGHTS

It's Monday. Your spouse is grouchy, your kids are sassy, and your neighbor complains about your barking dog. Real-life situations often call for supernatural responses. Through prayer and Holy Spirit power, with the Lord as your strength and your guide, as you obey Him, you can rest assured that the words of your mouth and meditations of your heart will be acceptable to Him. Even in real-life conflicts. Even on Monday.

YOUR THOUGHTS

_____

_____

_____

_____

_____

_____

_____

_____

_____

TAKE AWAY

What have you learned or re-thought that will enhance your walk with the Lord today?

_____

_____

_____

PRAY

_____

_____

_____

OBEY

All day. You can do it because He will do it through you if you let Him.

DAY 57: The Christian Inheritance

...to an inheritance incorruptible and undefiled and that does not fade away, reserved in heaven for you who are kept by the power of God through faith for salvation ready to be revealed the last time.

I Peter 1:4-5

OBSERVE

Check the traits this scripture invokes:

Courage? _____   Boldness? _____   Honor? _____

Steadfastness? _____   Other? _____

MY THOUGHTS

You, as a born-again believer, have a great inheritance reserved for you in heaven. Meanwhile, you must live your life on earth. Christ came that you might have an abundant life *(John 10:10)*. That spiritual abundance began at the moment of your salvation and will continue through eternity. Through the power of the Holy Spirit, you can feast on God's blessings every day without diminishing your inheritance by a crumb.

YOUR THOUGHTS

_____

_____

_____

_____

_____

_____

_____

TAKE AWAY

What have you learned or re-thought that will enhance your walk with the Lord today?

_____

_____

_____

PRAY

_____

_____

_____

OBEY

All day. You can do it because He will do it through you if you let Him.

DAY 58: Time and Times

I say, "You are my God; my times are in Your hands."
Psalm 31:14b, 15a

OBSERVE

Check the traits this scripture invokes:

Courage? _____   Boldness? _____   Honor? _____

Steadfastness? _____   Other? _____

MY THOUGHTS

My "time", the length of my life, is in God's hands, and I can neither lengthen nor shorten my life as God knows it to be. But my "times," my day-to-day life, my choices, my decisions, these things I could put into my own hands, not seeking God's will nor His wisdom. Such self-will is almost doomed to failure, and it might make my "time" shorter than it would have been if I had put my "times" in His hands, as the psalmist did.

YOUR THOUGHTS

_____

_____

_____

_____

_____

_____

_____

_____

_____

TAKE AWAY

What have you learned or re-thought that will enhance your walk with the Lord today?

_____

_____

_____

PRAY

_____

_____

_____

OBEY

All day. You can do it because He will do it through you if you let Him.

DAY 59: Courage, Strength, and Hope

Be of good courage, and He shall strengthen your heart,
all you who hope in the Lord.
Psalm 31:24

OBSERVE

Check the traits this scripture invokes:

Courage? _____   Boldness? _____   Honor? _____

Steadfastness? _____   Other? _____

MY THOUGHTS

This verse, in reverse order, says that if you put your hope in the Lord, He will give you internal strength, which gives you courage. You do not have to fret and fear and work up strength and courage on your own. Fully trust in the Lord, and He will give you true courage. And as He strengthens your heart, He may even soften it.

YOUR THOUGHTS

_____

_____

_____

_____

_____

_____

_____

_____

_____

TAKE AWAY

What have you learned or re-thought that will enhance your walk with the Lord today?

_____

_____

_____

PRAY

_____

_____

_____

OBEY

All day. You can do it because He will do it through you if you let Him.

DAY 60: Truth and Wisdom

*Behold, You desire truth in the inward
parts, and in the hidden part,
You will make me to know wisdom.*
Psalm 51:6

OBSERVE

Check the traits this scripture invokes:

Courage? _____   Boldness? _____   Honor? _____

Steadfastness? _____   Other? _____

MY THOUGHTS

You can fill your mind and your brain with much knowledge, which you should do. You should always be learning. But knowledge does not make you wise. Wisdom lives as truth in your heart, your soul, your spirit—in the hidden parts. Wisdom is not something that you can acquire on your own; it is a gift of God, and it is exhibited when you, in faith, act on the truth God reveals to you. Wisdom is God in action. And that is the truth.

YOUR THOUGHTS

_____

_____

_____

_____

_____

_____

_____

_____

_____

TAKE AWAY

What have you learned or re-thought that will enhance your walk with the Lord today?

_____

_____

_____

PRAY

_____

_____

_____

OBEY

All day. You can do it because He will do it through you if you let Him.

DAY 61: Pride vs. Humility

*When pride comes, then comes shame, but
with the humble is wisdom.*
Proverbs 11:2

OBSERVE

Check the traits this scripture invokes:

Courage? ____   Boldness? ____   Honor? ____

Steadfastness? ____   Other? _____

MY THOUGHTS

The humble person knows the wisdom of *Let another praise you,
and not your own mouth… (Proverbs 27:2)*. But the conceited,
the egotists, the braggarts, in their pride dismiss this verse as
a verse for the weak. Lives built on such foolish pride are on a
shaky foundation. What a shame.

YOUR THOUGHTS

_____

_____

_____

_____

_____

_____

_____

_____

_____

TAKE AWAY

What have you learned or re-thought that will enhance your walk with the Lord today?

_____

_____

_____

PRAY

_____

_____

_____

OBEY

All day. You can do it because He will do it through you if you let Him.

DAY 62: Not Like a Pauper

And in Your majesty, ride prosperously, because
of truth, humility, and righteousness.

Psalm 45:4(a)

OBSERVE

Check the traits this scripture invokes:

Courage? _____   Boldness? _____   Honor? _____

Steadfastness? _____   Other? _____

MY THOUGHTS

Scholars say that this Psalm speaks of the majestic Messiah and His Bride, the Church. As a Christian, you are a part of the Church; but you are also a child of the King. Let His royal life of truth, humility and righteousness be yours as He lives His life through you. You may be poor, but you are not a pauper. Live and act like the Messiah's bride or the King's kid: truthful, humble, righteous, and valiant. That is true majesty.

YOUR THOUGHTS

_____

_____

_____

_____

_____

TAKE AWAY

What have you learned or re-thought that will enhance your walk with the Lord today?

_____

_____

_____

PRAY

_____

_____

_____

OBEY

All day. You can do it because He will do it through you if you let Him.

DAY 63: Burden-sharing

Come to Me, all you who labor and are heavy-leaden, and I will give you rest. Take My yoke upon you and learn from Me, for I am gentle and lowly in heart, and you will find rest for your souls. For My yoke is easy, and My burden is light.
Matthew 11:28-30

OBSERVE

Check the traits this scripture invokes:

Courage? _____   Boldness? _____   Honor? _____

Steadfastness? _____   Other? _____

MY THOUGHTS

You can learn *about* Jesus by reading about Him and by listening to people preach and teach about Him. But you can learn *from* Him only by personal experience. Ask the Holy Spirit to live out His life through your life and to put you under His easy yoke of love, mercy, and justice. He doesn't say your circumstances will change; they may, but whether they do or not, He says you will change. You will have rest in your soul.

YOUR THOUGHTS

_____

_____

_____

_____

_____

_____

_____

_____

_____

TAKE AWAY

What have you learned or re-thought that will enhance your walk with the Lord today?

_____

_____

_____

PRAY

_____

_____

_____

OBEY

All day. You can do it because He will do it through you if you let Him.

DAY 64: Whom Will You Serve?

… choose for yourselves this day whom you will serve…
Joshua 24:15a

OBSERVE

Check the traits this scripture invokes:

Courage? _____   Boldness? _____   Honor? _____

Steadfastness? _____   Other? _____

MY THOUGHTS

You can say that you believe in Jesus and yet, serve the devil. True belief, faith, lies in the heart and results in service, in life action. If Jesus has no part in your life, you might wish to re-think your salvation. Because if you are not serving Jesus, you are serving the devil. There is no in-between. It is your choice.

YOUR THOUGHTS

_____

_____

_____

_____

_____

_____

_____

_____

_____

TAKE AWAY

What have you learned or re-thought that will enhance your walk with the Lord today?

_____

_____

_____

PRAY

_____

_____

_____

OBEY

All day. You can do it because He will do it through you if you let Him.

DAY 65: You and Your House

...but as for me and my house, we will serve the Lord.
Joshua 24:15c

OBSERVE

Check the traits this scripture invokes:

Courage? _____   Boldness? _____   Honor? _____

Steadfastness? _____   Other? _____

MY THOUGHTS

If you are the head of your household, you, as the family leader, have an obligation to teach your family members about the Lord, about salvation, and about Christian living. You must also show them by example how to serve. As you lead them, serve them. That is what Jesus did. And let them serve you, lest they become lazy and selfish. You cannot truly serve God without serving others. Serving begins at home. Mutually.

YOUR THOUGHTS

_____

_____

_____

_____

_____

_____

_____

_____

_____

TAKE AWAY

What have you learned or re-thought that will enhance your walk with the Lord today?

_____

_____

_____

PRAY

_____

_____

_____

OBEY

All day. You can do it because He will do it through you if you let Him.

DAY 66: A Healthy Portion

*My flesh and my heart fail; but God is the strength
of my heart and my portion forever.*
Psalm 73:26

OBSERVE

Check the traits this scripture invokes:

Courage? _____   Boldness? _____   Honor? _____

Steadfastness? _____   Other? _____

MY THOUGHTS

When you are young and unafraid, bold, strong, and confident
in yourself, that is the time when you should put your hope and
trust in the Lord, making His strength your strength, enhancing
your natural emotions. Then, when your flesh and your heart
fail—and they will—you need not fear and beg for God; He is
already there as the strength of your heart; He is your portion,
your inheritance. Forever. And He never fails.

YOUR THOUGHTS

_____

_____

_____

_____

_____

_____

_____

_____

_____

TAKE AWAY

What have you learned or re-thought that will enhance your walk with the Lord today?

_____

_____

_____

PRAY

_____

_____

_____

OBEY

All day. You can do it because He will do it through you if you let Him.

DAY 67: The Prayer of the Upright

The sacrifice of the wicked is an abomination to the Lord,
but the prayer of the upright is His delight.
Proverbs 15:8

OBSERVE

Check the traits this scripture invokes:

Courage? _____ Boldness? _____ Honor? _____

Steadfastness? _____ Other? _____

MY THOUGHTS

God hates sin, and if you are living in sin, you cannot buy God's favor, neither with money nor sacrifice. He does not want your penance; He wants your repentance. Sometimes, it takes a lot of courage to repent. But repentance pays big dividends, one of them being that your prayers will be a delight to God. When you make God happy, He makes you happy. That is delightful.

YOUR THOUGHTS

_____

_____

_____

_____

_____

_____

_____

_____

_____

TAKE AWAY

What have you learned or re-thought that will enhance your walk with the Lord today?

_____

_____

_____

PRAY

_____

_____

_____

OBEY

All day. You can do it because He will do it through you if you let Him.

DAY 68: The Word of the Lord

But the word of the Lord endures forever.
I Peter 1:25

OBSERVE

Check the traits this scripture invokes:

Courage? _____   Boldness? _____   Honor? _____

Steadfastness? _____   Other? _____

MY THOUGHTS

Life is a series of never-ending changes. Some are good; some are destructive. That is why in the throes of social, moral, cultural, and political changes, one must evaluate such changes by scripture, not by public opinion. Opinions change and civilizations fall, but the word of the Lord never changes. It endures forever.

YOUR THOUGHTS

_____

_____

_____

_____

_____

_____

_____

_____

_____

TAKE AWAY

What have you learned or re-thought that will enhance your walk with the Lord today?

_____

_____

_____

PRAY

_____

_____

_____

OBEY

All day. You can do it because He will do it through you if you let Him.

DAY 69: Pass It On

That the generation to come might know them [**God's laws**]
... that they may set their hope in God and not forget the
works of God, but keep His commandments, and may not be
like their fathers, a stubborn and rebellious generation.
Psalm 78:6a, 7, 8a

OBSERVE

Check the traits this scripture invokes:

Courage? _____   Boldness? _____   Honor? _____

Steadfastness? _____   Other? _____

MY THOUGHTS

This is your time: your time to teach the next generation that
they can live lives that far surpass yours. When you are stubborn
and rebellious, repent at once, and let the next generation see the
victorious change in your life and attitude. Pray that your children
and their families will live more godly lives than you have lived;
and pray that they will pray this same prayer for their children.

YOUR THOUGHTS

_____

_____

_____

_____

_____

_____

_____

_____

_____

TAKE AWAY

What have you learned or re-thought that will enhance your walk with the Lord today?

_____

_____

_____

PRAY

_____

_____

_____

OBEY

All day. You can do it because He will do it through you if you let Him.

DAY 70: What Does the Lord Require?

*But as He who called you is holy, you also
be holy in all your conduct,
because it is written, "Be holy, for I am holy."*
I Peter 1:15, 16

OBSERVE

Check the traits this scripture invokes:

Courage? _____   Boldness? _____   Honor? _____

Steadfastness? _____   Other? _____

MY THOUGHTS

God, the Holy Spirit within your heart, makes you holy. All you must do is obey. Micah 6:8 says *"...what does the Lord require of you: but to do justly, to love mercy, and to walk humbly with your God."* Do these things in your daily life and that will set you apart from the mass of people, making you worthy of respect; that is what it means to be holy: set apart and worthy of respect. Holy, but not "holier than thou."

YOUR THOUGHTS

_____

_____

_____

_____

_____

_____

_____

_____

_____

TAKE AWAY

What have you learned or re-thought that will enhance your walk with the Lord today?

_____

_____

_____

PRAY

_____

_____

_____

OBEY

All day. You can do it because He will do it through you if you let Him.

DAY 71: Being Ready: A Daily Discipline

Then I said, "Here am I! Send me."
Isaiah 6:8c

OBSERVE

Check the traits this scripture invokes:

Courage? _____   Boldness? _____   Honor? _____

Steadfastness? _____   Other? _____

MY THOUGHTS

Are you ready? Are you in good physical shape; are you doing your daily "to do's"; are your relationships right; are your loved ones secure in your love and God's love; are you emotionally prepared to do lowly tasks? If God called today, would you have to say, "Here am I, send me next month," or perhaps "Here am I, send George." Being ready to go takes much work each day; so does being ready to stay. Be prepared. To go or to stay.

YOUR THOUGHTS

_____

_____

_____

_____

_____

_____

_____

_____

_____

TAKE AWAY

What have you learned or re-thought that will enhance your walk with the Lord today?

_____

_____

_____

PRAY

_____

_____

_____

OBEY

All day. You can do it because He will do it through you if you let Him.

DAY 72: The Taste of Grace

*Therefore, laying aside all malice, all deceit, hypocrisy,
envy, and all evil speaking, as newborn babes, desire the
pure milk of the word, that you may grow thereby,
if indeed you have tasted that the Lord is gracious.*

I Peter 2:1-3

OBSERVE
Check the traits this scripture invokes:

Courage? _____   Boldness? _____   Honor? _____

Steadfastness? _____   Other? _____

MY THOUGHTS
If you are not growing spiritually, you may need to change your spiritual diet. Make sure you eliminate malice, deceit, hypocrisy, envy, and all evil speaking. They poison not only your spiritual system, but your mental and emotional systems as well. Feast daily on the milk of scripture, and you will soon hunger for meatier truths which will build spiritual muscle. That is, if you have truly tasted God's gracious salvation.

YOUR THOUGHTS

_____

_____

_____

_____

_____

_____

_____

_____

_____

TAKE AWAY

What have you learned or re-thought that will enhance your walk with the Lord today?

_____

_____

_____

PRAY

_____

_____

_____

OBEY

All day. You can do it because He will do it through you if you let Him.

DAY 73: Lending to the Lord

He who has pity on the poor lends to the Lord,
and He will pay back what he has given.
Proverbs 19:17

OBSERVE

Check the traits this scripture invokes:

Courage? _____   Boldness? _____   Honor? _____

Steadfastness? _____   Other? _____

MY THOUGHTS

Giving to the poor, whether it be food, clothing, financial aid, spiritual and emotional comfort, or any other aid, is like giving a loan to the Lord. He never fails to pay back. Payment is never late. Interest is always prime. (**Caveat:** *Though I bestow all my goods to feed the poor… and have not love, it profits me nothing.* See I Corinthians 13 for the part love plays. It will enhance your living. And probably your giving).

YOUR THOUGHTS

_____

_____

_____

_____

_____

_____

_____

_____

_____

TAKE AWAY

What have you learned or re-thought that will enhance your walk with the Lord today?

_____

_____

_____

PRAY

_____

_____

_____

OBEY

All day. You can do it because He will do it through you if you let Him.

DAY 74: God's Enduring Truth

For the Lord is good; His mercy is everlasting,
and His truth endures to all generations.

Psalm 100:5

OBSERVE

Check the traits this scripture invokes:

Courage? _____   Boldness? _____   Honor? _____

Steadfastness? _____   Other? _____

MY THOUGHTS

If you live by God's unchanging truth in a changing culture, you may be ridiculed and treated without mercy. But God's everlasting mercy will enable you through the power of the Holy Spirit to be valiant in a world that may be vicious toward you. In the hard times, the Lord is good. He is also good in the not-so-hard-times. And in the good times. In fact, God is good all the time. And that is the everlasting truth.

YOUR THOUGHTS

_____

_____

_____

_____

_____

_____

_____

_____

_____

TAKE AWAY

What have you learned or re-thought that will enhance your walk with the Lord today?

_____

_____

_____

PRAY

_____

_____

_____

OBEY

All day. You can do it because He will do it through you if you let Him.

DAY 75: The House on The Rock

Coming to Him as to a Living Stone, rejected indeed by men,
but chosen by God and precious,
you also as living stones are being built up a spiritual house…
I Peter 2:4, 5a

OBSERVE

Check the traits this scripture invokes:

Courage? _____   Boldness? _____   Honor? _____

Steadfastness? _____   Other? _____

MY THOUGHTS

Your spiritual house is being built on Christ. Being built by Him. With Him. For Him. The world may reject you. It rejected Jesus. But He, the Living Stone, is also your Living Hope. With the Living Stone as your foundation, your structure, and your hope, the scripture says that you, also, are living stones. And since you, like Christ, were chosen by God, your life can be as solid as a rock.

YOUR THOUGHTS

_____

_____

_____

_____

_____

_____

_____

_____

_____

TAKE AWAY

What have you learned or re-thought that will enhance your walk with the Lord today?

_____

_____

_____

PRAY

_____

_____

_____

OBEY

All day. You can do it because He will do it through you if you let Him.

DAY 76: Love: The Sacrificial Principle

You, also, as living stones, are being built up
a spiritual house, a holy priesthood,
to offer up spiritual sacrifices acceptable
to God through Jesus Christ.
I Peter 2:5

OBSERVE

Check the traits this scripture invokes:

Courage? _____   Boldness? _____   Honor? _____

Steadfastness? _____   Other? _____

MY THOUGHTS

As a Christian, you need no intermediary, other than Jesus Christ, to offer up spiritual sacrifices to God. Make sure that whatever you offer, praise, thanksgiving, intercession, money, are not just mere words nor actions done out of duty, guilt, or habit. Anything offered to God should be love-based: love of God and love of others. Otherwise, it is just noise or clutter. Not acceptable.

YOUR THOUGHTS

_____

_____

_____

_____

_____

_____

_____

_____

TAKE AWAY

What have you learned or re-thought that will enhance your walk with the Lord today

_____

_____

_____

PRAY

_____

_____

_____

OBEY

All day. You can do it because He will do it through you if you let Him.

DAY 77: After You Die, What About Your Children?

The righteous man walks in his integrity;
his children are blessed after him.

Proverbs 20:7

OBSERVE

Check the traits this scripture invokes:

Courage? ____   Boldness? ____   Honor? ____

Steadfastness? ____   Other? _____

MY THOUGHTS

The way to ensure that your children are blessed after you die is this: live a righteous life. You may or may not leave them a fortune, but if through Christ, you have walked in integrity, God will bless them with good and perfect gifts. *Every good gift and every perfect gift is from above and comes down from the Father of lights... (James 1:17).* Have a good walk. Your children are right behind you.

YOUR THOUGHTS

_____

_____

_____

_____

_____

_____

_____

_____

_____

TAKE AWAY

What have you learned or re-thought that will enhance your walk with the Lord today?

_____

_____

_____

PRAY

_____

_____

_____

OBEY

All day. You can do it because He will do it through you if you let Him.

DAY 78: How Do You Look?

The one who has a haughty look and a proud heart, him I will not endure.
Psalm 101:5b.
A haughty look, a proud heart, and the plowing of the wicked are sin.
Proverbs 21:4.
A proud and haughty man – "scoffer" is his name. He acts with arrogant pride.
Proverbs 21:24

OBSERVE

Check the traits this scripture invokes:

Courage? _____   Boldness? _____   Honor? _____
Steadfastness? _____   Other? _____

MY THOUGHTS

These are only a few of the scriptures that warn against being proud and haughty. If your nose is in the air and your eyes are looking down on other people, beware. God says he will not endure such actions. He doesn't like sin—and yes, haughtiness is sin. So is arrogant pride. Look your best. but be careful how you look.

YOUR THOUGHTS

_____

_____

_____

_____

_____

_____

_____

_____

TAKE AWAY

What have you learned or re-thought that will enhance your walk with the Lord today?

_____

_____

_____

PRAY

_____

_____

_____

OBEY

All day. You can do it because He will do it through you if you let Him.

DAY 79: Things That Pertain to Life and Godliness

[…] as His divine power has given to us all things that
pertain to life and godliness through the knowledge
of Him who called us by glory and virtue.

II Peter 1:3

OBSERVE

Check the traits this scripture invokes:

Courage? _____   Boldness? _____   Honor? _____

Steadfastness? _____   Other? _____

MY THOUGHTS

If you are a believer, the Holy Spirit has already given to you everything you need to live a godly life. You simply need to access that treasure-trove by prayer and scripture study. Open the Book. Read the instructions. Pray for wisdom and understanding. And live your life accordingly. Every day. It is that simple.

YOUR THOUGHTS

_____

_____

_____

_____

_____

_____

_____

_____

_____

TAKE AWAY

What have you learned or re-thought that will enhance your walk with the Lord today?

_____

_____

_____

PRAY

_____

_____

_____

OBEY

All day. You can do it because He will do it through you if you let Him.

DAY 80: What is Right?

*In those days, there was no king in Israel; everyone
did what was right in his own eyes.*
Judges 21:25

OBSERVE

Check the traits this scripture invokes:

Courage? _____   Boldness? _____   Honor? _____

Steadfastness? _____   Other? _____

MY THOUGHTS

When everyone does "what is right in his own eyes," chaos is sure
to result. Guidelines are essential to live in unity. This is true in
families as well as in nations. God's word gives us clear standards
for living, and we have complete freedom to live as we wish
within God's boundaries. What a transformed world we would
have if everyone did what was right in God's eyes. Is that right?

YOUR THOUGHTS

_____

_____

_____

_____

_____

_____

_____

_____

_____

TAKE AWAY

What have you learned or re-thought that will enhance your walk with the Lord today?

_____

_____

_____

PRAY

_____

_____

_____

OBEY

All day. You can do it because He will do it through you if you let Him.

DAY 81: No Figs, No Fruit, No Flocks. Now What?

Though the fig tree may not blossom, nor fruit be on the vine; though the labor of the olive may fail, and the fields yield no food; though the flock be cut off from the fold, and there be no herd in the stalls — yet I will rejoice in the Lord. I will joy in the God of my salvation. The Lord God is my strength. He will make my feet like deer's feet, and He will make me walk on my high hills.
Habakkuk 3:17-19

OBSERVE

Check the traits this scripture invokes:

Courage? _____   Boldness? _____   Honor? _____

Steadfastness? _____   Other? _____

MY THOUGHTS

Rejoice: really rejoice! Find joy in God in the good times. Let Him be your strength during the times when you think you are on top of the world. Then, when hard, and even harder times occur, you will naturally turn to the Lord, not in panic, but in perfect faith that He, indeed, is the God of salvation and your strength; you know Him well. Rejoice, and He will keep you steady, as agile as a deer in the high hills, rejoicing all the more.

YOUR THOUGHTS

_____

_____

_____

_____

_____

_____

_____

TAKE AWAY

What have you learned or re-thought that will enhance your walk with the Lord today?

_____

_____

_____

PRAY

_____

_____

_____

OBEY

All day. You can do it because He will do it through you if you let Him.

DAY 82: Precious Thoughts

How precious also are Your thoughts to me, O
God! How great is the sum of them!
If I should count them, they would be
more in number than the sand.
Psalm 139:17, 18a

OBSERVE
Check the traits this scripture invokes:

Courage? _____   Boldness? _____   Honor? _____

Steadfastness? _____   Other? _____

MY THOUGHTS
More in number than the sand: those are a lot of thoughts! Jeremiah explains what some of these thoughts are: *"For I know the thoughts that I think toward you,"* says the Lord, *"thoughts of peace and not of evil, to give you a future and a hope" (Jeremiah 29:11).* Those thoughts were for Judah, but the principle applies to Christians today. Believe and obey. What could more precious than God's hope for your future? Think about that.

YOUR THOUGHTS

_____

_____

_____

_____

_____

_____

_____

_____

_____

TAKE AWAY

What have you learned or re-thought that will enhance your walk with the Lord today?

_____

_____

_____

PRAY

_____

_____

_____

OBEY

All day. You can do it because He will do it through you if you let Him.

DAY 83: In the Morning

My voice You shall hear in the morning, O Lord;
In the morning, I will direct it to You. And I will look up.
Psalm 5:3

OBSERVE

Check the traits this scripture invokes:

Courage? _____   Boldness? _____   Honor? _____

Steadfastness? _____   Other? _____

MY THOUGHTS

A morning prayer when you first arise helps put your spiritual metabolism to work. That morning prayer does not have to be long, just heart-felt, as you lift your words and your heart and your eyes to God. Praise, thanksgiving, supplication, or any other type of prayer will begin the process of putting spiritual power into your daily decisions. Look up.

YOUR THOUGHTS

_____

_____

_____

_____

_____

_____

_____

_____

_____

TAKE AWAY

What have you learned or re-thought that will enhance your walk with the Lord today?

_____

_____

_____

PRAY

_____

_____

_____

OBEY

All day. You can do it because He will do it through you if you let Him.

DAY 84: Confession: God's Bar of Soap

If we confess our sins, He is faithful and just to forgive us our sins and to cleanse us from all unrighteousness.

I John 1:9

OBSERVE

Check the traits this scripture invokes:

Courage? _____   Boldness? _____   Honor? _____

Steadfastness? _____   Other? _____

MY THOUGHTS

As soon as God convicts you that you have sinned, no matter how great or how small the sin, confess it immediately. God will forgive immediately. You will be spiritually clean immediately, and you will be free not to commit that sin again. Use God's bar of soap as often as you need it; you will be glad you did. So will the people around you.

YOUR THOUGHTS

_____

_____

_____

_____

_____

_____

_____

_____

_____

TAKE AWAY

What have you learned or re-thought that will enhance your walk with the Lord today?

_____

_____

_____

PRAY

_____

_____

_____

OBEY

All day. You can do it because He will do it through you if you let Him.

DAY 85: Abiding in Christ Jesus

And this is His commandment: that we should
believe on the name of His Son Jesus Christ and love
one another, as He gave us commandment.
Now he who keeps His commandments
abides in Him and He in him.
I John 3:23, 24a

OBSERVE

Check the traits this scripture invokes:

Courage? _____   Boldness? _____   Honor? _____

Steadfastness? _____   Other? _____

MY THOUGHTS

Everyone can love with human love, but only when we believe
on the name of His Son Jesus Christ can we love with the love
of God, because we have God living within our hearts. *And this
is His commandment, that we should believe on the name of His
Son Jesus Christ* (commandment to believe) *and love one another*
(commandment to love with His love). Summary: Believe on
Christ + Love others = Abide in Christ. And vice-versa.

YOUR THOUGHTS

_____

_____

_____

_____

_____

_____

_____

_____

TAKE AWAY

What have you learned or re-thought that will enhance your
walk with the Lord today?

_____

_____

_____

PRAY

_____

_____

_____

OBEY

All day. You can do it because He will do it through you if you
let Him.

DAY 86: How Firm a Foundation

If the foundations are destroyed, what can the righteous do?
Psalm 11:3

OBSERVE

Check the traits this scripture invokes:

Courage? _____   Boldness? _____   Honor? _____

Steadfastness? _____   Other? _____

MY THOUGHTS

Nations tumble and civilizations crumble, but the Lord and His word stand forever. When everything about you seems to be in chaos, stand firm in your faith. The time to be valiant is when foundations around you are crumbling. With Christ as your foundation, you will never be destroyed. For even though you die, you will live forever. That is a foundational truth that will never be destroyed.

YOUR THOUGHTS

_____

_____

_____

_____

_____

_____

_____

_____

_____

TAKE AWAY

What have you learned or re-thought that will enhance your
walk with the Lord today?

_____

_____

_____

PRAY

_____

_____

_____

OBEY

All day. You can do it because He will do it through you if you
let Him.

DAY 87: The Prosperous Soul

Beloved, I pray that you may prosper in all things and be in health, just as your soul prospers.
III John 1:2

OBSERVE
Check the traits this scripture invokes:

Courage? _____   Boldness? _____   Honor? _____

Steadfastness? _____   Other? _____

MY THOUGHTS
As you pray for the financial success and the physical and emotional well-being of those you love, do not fail to pray for their spiritual victories. The soul grows on spiritual food, such as prayer and Bible study. But it is in the winning of spiritual battles, such as overcoming temptations and being obedient to God's directions, that the soul prospers. Such winning takes personal courage and action, including action of the will.

YOUR THOUGHTS

_____

_____

_____

_____

_____

_____

_____

_____

_____

TAKE AWAY

What have you learned or re-thought that will enhance your
walk with the Lord today?

_____

_____

_____

PRAY

_____

_____

_____

OBEY

All day. You can do it because He will do it through you if you
let Him.

DAY 88: A Parent's Greatest Joy

I have no greater joy than to hear that
my children walk in the truth.
III John 1:4

OBSERVE

Check the traits this scripture invokes:

Courage? ____   Boldness? ____   Honor? ____

Steadfastness? ____   Other? _____

MY THOUGHTS

When one truly walks in the truth, he or she walks in the Truth, because Jesus said, *"I am the Way, The Truth, and the Life" (John 14:6)*. Nothing should make parents happier than to know their children are walking in the truth and, thus, in the Truth. Everything else takes second place to this greatest joy. Do your children know that?

YOUR THOUGHTS

_____

_____

_____

_____

_____

_____

_____

_____

_____

TAKE AWAY

What have you learned or re-thought that will enhance your walk with the Lord today?

_____

_____

_____

PRAY

_____

_____

_____

OBEY

All day. You can do it because He will do it through you if you let Him.

DAY 89: The Way the Lord Works

"For the oppression of the poor, for the sighing
of the needy, Now I will arise,"
says the Lord; "I will set him in the safety for which he yearns."
Psalm 12:5

OBSERVE

Check the traits this scripture invokes:

Courage? _____   Boldness? _____   Honor? _____

Steadfastness? _____   Other? _____

MY THOUGHTS

Perhaps the Lord wants to use you to set some poor, needy soul *in the safety in which he yearns*. Using ordinary people to accomplish extraordinary things is the way the Lord often works. But don't be anxious. If He calls on you, He will equip and supply you with everything you need. That is the way the Lord always works. Are you listening?

YOUR THOUGHTS

_____

_____

_____

_____

_____

_____

_____

_____

_____

TAKE AWAY

What have you learned or re-thought that will enhance your walk with the Lord today?

_____

_____

_____

PRAY

_____

_____

_____

OBEY

All day. You can do it because He will do it through you if you let Him.

DAY 90: The Fear of the Lord

*Only fear the Lord and serve Him in truth with all your heart;
for consider what great things He has done for you.*
I Samuel 12:24

OBSERVE
Check the traits this scripture invokes:

Courage? _____   Boldness? _____   Honor? _____

Steadfastness? _____   Other? _____

MY THOUGHTS
To fear the Lord is to love, honor, worship, and obey Him when everything is going your way and when nothing is going your way. Circumstances change, but they do not change the way God loves you, nor should they change the way you love God. He has done great things for you, the greatest being your salvation. That truly deserves your love, honor, worship, and obedience. That is fearing the Lord, without being afraid of Him.

YOUR THOUGHTS

_____

_____

_____

_____

_____

_____

_____

_____

_____

TAKE AWAY

What have you learned or re-thought that will enhance your walk with the Lord today?

_____

_____

_____

PRAY

_____

_____

_____

OBEY

All day. You can do it because He will do it through you if you let Him.

DAY 91: Troubling Times

God is our refuge and strength, a very present help in trouble.
Therefore, we will not fear, even though the earth be
removed, and though the mountains be carried into the
midst of the sea, though its waters roar and be troubled,
though the mountains shake with its swelling.
Psalm 46:1-3

OBSERVE

Check the traits this scripture invokes:

Courage? _____   Boldness? _____   Honor? _____

Steadfastness? _____   Other? _____

MY THOUGHTS

Help is not on the way. Help is here! God, a very present help in time of trouble, and is waiting for you to call out to Him. He will answer. Right away. It might not be the answer you want, but it will be the answer that is best for you and God's purpose. Give Him your fears and He will give you His peace in knowing He truly is in control, even in the situations we hate. Even in earthquakes, hurricanes, and solar disruptions.

YOUR THOUGHTS

_____

_____

_____

_____

_____

_____

_____

_____

_____

TAKE AWAY

What have you learned or re-thought that will enhance your walk with the Lord today?

_____

_____

_____

PRAY

_____

_____

_____

OBEY

All day. You can do it because He will do it through you if you let Him.

DAY 92: Almost Obedient

Then Saul said to Samuel, "I have sinned, for I have
transgressed the commandment of the Lord and your words,
because I feared the people and obeyed their voice."
I Samuel 15:24

OBSERVE
Check the traits this scripture invokes:

Courage? _____   Boldness? _____   Honor? _____

Steadfastness? _____   Other? _____

MY THOUGHTS
Saul feared his people and gave in to their demands rather than completely obeying God, and God ultimately took away his kingship. Saul was almost obedient. But "almost" doesn't win God's favor, neither in Old Testament conflicts nor in twenty-first century cultural wars. When culture and public opinion demand one thing and the word of God demands another, go with God.

YOUR THOUGHTS
_____
_____
_____
_____

_____

_____

_____

_____

_____

TAKE AWAY

What have you learned or re-thought that will enhance your walk with the Lord today?

_____

_____

_____

PRAY

_____

_____

_____

OBEY

All day. You can do it because He will do it through you if you let Him.

DAY 93: Fluff and Stuff

They are clouds without water, carried about by the winds.
Jude 1:12b

OBSERVE

Check the traits this scripture invokes:

Courage? _____   Boldness? _____   Honor? _____

Steadfastness? _____   Other? _____

MY THOUGHTS

Big, fluffy, white clouds are beautiful to see but they offer little or no water. Cotton candy is sweet to the taste, but it offers little or no food value. Eloquent and emotionally compelling sermons may be delightful to hear, but if they are not focused on the word of God, they offer little or no substance. Beware of spiritual fluff.

YOUR THOUGHTS

_____

_____

_____

_____

_____

_____

_____

_____

_____

TAKE AWAY

What have you learned or re-thought that will enhance your walk with the Lord today?

_____

_____

_____

PRAY

_____

_____

_____

OBEY

All day. You can do it because He will do it through you if you let Him.

DAY 94: In the Name Of....

For all people walk each in the name of his god.
But we will walk in the name of the Lord
our God forever and ever.
Micah 4:5

OBSERVE

Check the traits this scripture invokes:

Courage? _____   Boldness? _____   Honor? _____

Steadfastness? _____   Other? _____

MY THOUGHTS

Everybody has a god, even the atheists who say, "God is dead."
What is the name of your god? Buddha. Baha'i. Nature. Money.
Sports. Work. Science. Self. The list goes on and on. But only the
name of the Lord our God (Father, Son, and Holy Spirit) lives
forever. If you are not walking in His name, now is a good time
to start. Trust in Him and let Him set the pace. And live forever.

YOUR THOUGHTS

_____

_____

_____

_____

_____

_____

_____

_____

_____

TAKE AWAY

What have you learned or re-thought that will enhance your walk with the Lord today?

_____

_____

_____

PRAY

_____

_____

_____

OBEY

All day. You can do it because He will do it through you if you let Him.

DAY 95: The Good Life

Who is the man who desires life, and loves
many days, that he may see good?
Keep your tongue from evil, and your lips from speaking deceit.
Depart from evil and do good. Seek peace and pursue it.
Psalm 34:12-14

OBSERVE

Check the traits this scripture invokes:

Courage? _____   Boldness? _____   Honor? _____

Steadfastness? _____   Other? _____

MY THOUGHTS

Wealth and power, fortune and fame are not the determining factors for the good life. The good life means to speak the truth; be honest; do good deeds; be a peacemaker. Or as Christ said, "*...seek first the kingdom of God and His righteousness, and all these (other) things shall be added unto you*" (*Matthew 6:33*). That is the good life.

YOUR THOUGHTS

_____

_____

_____

_____

_____

_____

_____

_____

_____

TAKE AWAY

What have you learned or re-thought that will enhance your walk with the Lord today?

_____

_____

_____

PRAY

_____

_____

_____

OBEY

All day. You can do it because He will do it through you if you let Him.

DAY 96: Watch Your Step

Now to Him who is able to keep you from
stumbling, and to present you faultless before the
presence of His glory with exceeding joy, ...
Jude 1:24

OBSERVE

Check the traits this scripture invokes:

Courage? _____   Boldness? _____   Honor? _____

Steadfastness? _____   Other? _____

MY THOUGHTS

Handrails and grab-bars will help to keep you from stumbling physically. So watch your step, and grab on to them when they are available. Not only can the Lord keep you from stumbling spiritually, but He will also present you in perfect spiritual condition when you appear before the Father. So watch your step, grab onto Him, and hold on with a tight grasp. That will fill Him with joy. And He is always within easy reach.

YOUR THOUGHTS

_____

_____

_____

_____

_____

_____

_____

_____

_____

TAKE AWAY

What have you learned or re-thought that will enhance your walk with the Lord today?

_____

_____

_____

PRAY

_____

_____

_____

OBEY

All day. You can do it because He will do it through you if you let Him.

DAY 97: "The Good Ole' Days"

Now the Lord said to Samuel, "How long will you mourn for Saul,
seeing I have rejected him from reigning over Israel?
Fill your horn with oil and go… for I have
provided Myself a king among his sons"
I Samuel 16:1

OBSERVE

Check the traits this scripture invokes:

Courage? _____   Boldness? _____   Honor? _____

Steadfastness? _____ Other? _____

MY THOUGHTS

The good ole' days are gone. Forever. Remember them, but don't mourn them. God is at work right now, even amid ungodly conflict and cultural turmoil. He has a purpose, and He will accomplish that purpose in His time, just as He did in Saul's and David's time. Meanwhile, have faith, persevere, not mourning for what was, but letting God use you right now in the "what is."

YOUR THOUGHTS

_____

_____

_____

_____

_____

_____

_____

_____

_____

TAKE AWAY

What have you learned or re-thought that will enhance your walk with the Lord today?

_____

_____

_____

PRAY

_____

_____

_____

OBEY

All day. You can do it because He will do it through you if you let Him.

DAY 98: Let Go

*I sought the Lord, and He heard me, and
delivered me from all my fears.*
Psalm 34:4

OBSERVE

Check the traits this scripture invokes:

Courage? _____   Boldness? _____   Honor? _____

Steadfastness? _____   Other? _____

MY THOUGHTS

If left unchecked, fear always wins. Fear disables; fear cripples;
fear destroys. God will take away our fears, but only if we ask
Him to take them; then we must let go of them. He will not take
them by force. Without fear, we can face our enemies, whatever
or whoever they may be, and with Christ as our strength, we will
be victorious. Because Christ is never fearful, and He is always
victorious. Even in death.

YOUR THOUGHTS

_____

_____

_____

_____

_____

_____

_____

_____

_____

TAKE AWAY

What have you learned or re-thought that will enhance your walk with the Lord today?

_____

_____

_____

PRAY

_____

_____

_____

OBEY

All day. You can do it because He will do it through you if you let Him.

DAY 99: Good and Happy

He who heeds the word wisely will find good,
And whoever trusts in the Lord, happy is he.
Proverbs 16:20

OBSERVE

Check the traits this scripture invokes:

Courage? _____   Boldness? _____   Honor? _____

Steadfastness? _____   Other? _____

MY THOUGHTS

When the Lord speaks to you through His word, how do you "heed the word wisely?" You simply believe what it says and do what the Lord tells you to do. It may not always be easy, but it is always possible. Because, as it says in *Philippians 4:13, I can do all things* (that He tells me to do) *through Christ, who strengthens me.* So, the conclusion is this: heed the word and trust the Lord. That will make you happy. And happiness is a pretty good find.

YOUR THOUGHTS

_____

_____

_____

_____

_____

_____

_____

_____

_____

TAKE AWAY

What have you learned or re-thought that will enhance your walk with the Lord today?

_____

_____

_____

PRAY

_____

_____

_____

OBEY

All day. You can do it because He will do it through you if you let Him.

DAY 100: Choices

*Commit your works to the Lord, and your
thoughts will be established.*
Proverbs 16:3

OBSERVE

Check the traits this scripture invokes:

Courage? _____   Boldness? _____   Honor? _____

Steadfastness? _____   Other? _____

MY THOUGHTS

In the morning. That's when it should start. The commitment
of your works (your actions, your words, your thoughts) to the
Lord should start in the morning. Ask Him to set the course for
the day, and He will do it. But He won't force you to follow it.
He will establish your thoughts, but it is your choice to follow or
not. Think about that.

YOUR THOUGHTS

_____

_____

_____

_____

_____

_____

_____

_____

_____

TAKE AWAY

What have you learned or re-thought that will enhance your walk with the Lord today?

_____

_____

_____

PRAY

_____

_____

_____

OBEY

All day. You can do it because He will do it through you if you let Him.

DAY 101: What's It Worth?

How much better to get wisdom than gold!
And to get understanding is to be chosen rather than silver.
Proverbs 16:16

OBSERVE

Check the traits this scripture invokes:

Courage? _____   Boldness? _____   Honor? _____

Steadfastness? _____   Other? _____

MY THOUGHTS

You cannot place a monetary value on wisdom and understanding; they soar above worldly knowledge and logic, and they plunge deeper than social justice and equity. *The fear of the Lord is the beginning of wisdom, and knowledge of the Holy One is understanding (Proverbs 9:10).* For you to know God costs you nothing; for you to know God cost Christ His life. When you understand this, you are very wise. And rich.

YOUR THOUGHTS

_____

_____

_____

_____

_____

_____

_____

_____

_____

TAKE AWAY

What have you learned or re-thought that will enhance your walk with the Lord today?

_____

_____

_____

PRAY

_____

_____

_____

OBEY

All day. You can do it because He will do it through you if you let Him.

DAY 102: A Big Appetite

I am the Lord your God who brought you out of the land of Egypt;
open your mouth wide, and I will fill it.

Psalm 81:10

OBSERVE

Check the traits this scripture invokes:

Courage? _____   Boldness? _____   Honor? _____

Steadfastness? _____   Other? _____

MY THOUGHTS

You can boldly ask the Lord in prayer for specific needs or blessings; or you can boldly pray for and receive those things which He wants to give you. Either way, you can be assured that when you depend upon God, and tell Him so, and when you are obedient and hunger and thirst after righteousness, you can expect Him to feed you. With His food. Open your mouth wide. Let Him know how hungry you are.

YOUR THOUGHTS

_____

_____

_____

_____

_____

_____

_____

_____

_____

TAKE AWAY

What have you learned or re-thought that will enhance your
walk with the Lord today?

_____

_____

_____

PRAY

_____

_____

_____

OBEY

All day. You can do it because He will do it through you if you
let Him.

DAY 103: Jesus' Prayer

(Jesus praying): I do not pray that You
should take them out of the world,
but that You should keep them from the evil one.
John 17:15

OBSERVE

Check the traits this scripture invokes:

Courage? _____   Boldness? _____   Honor? _____

Steadfastness? _____   Other? _____

MY THOUGHTS

It should not be a balancing act to live in the world, but not of the world. Rather, it should be an act of remembering Jesus' prayer, claiming it for your own life, trusting God to answer that prayer, and living like you believe it. That is valiant living. Joyful living. In the world. Because of Jesus' prayer and your obedience.

YOUR THOUGHTS

_____

_____

_____

_____

_____

_____

_____

_____

_____

TAKE AWAY

What have you learned or re-thought that will enhance your walk with the Lord today?

_____

_____

_____

PRAY

_____

_____

_____

OBEY

All day. You can do it because He will do it through you if you let Him.

DAY 104: What's Lacking?

We urge you, brethren, that you increase
more and more [in brotherly love];
that you also aspire to lead a quiet life, to mind your own business,
and to work with your own hands …
and that you may lack nothing.
I Thessalonians 4:10c, 11, 12b

OBSERVE
Check the traits this scripture invokes:

Courage? _____   Boldness? _____   Honor? _____

Steadfastness? _____   Other? _____

MY THOUGHTS
Leading a quiet life does not mean living a boring life, but it does mean minding your own business and being responsible in your work. These two simple things, couched in ever-increasing brotherly love, can help to erase your restless unease and insatiable desires and discontentment. That is peace of mind. That is the quiet life, even amid new adventures or tumultuous times.

YOUR THOUGHTS

_____

_____

_____

_____

_____

_____

_____

_____

_____

TAKE AWAY

What have you learned or re-thought that will enhance your walk with the Lord today?

_____

_____

_____

PRAY

_____

_____

_____

OBEY

All day. You can do it because He will do it through you if you let Him.

DAY 105: Repetition

The fear of the Lord is the beginning of wisdom;
a good understanding have all those who do His commandments.
Psalm 111:10a

OBSERVE

Check the traits this scripture invokes:

Courage? _____   Boldness? _____   Honor? _____

Steadfastness? _____   Other? _____

MY THOUGHTS

We talked about wisdom and understanding on Days 10, 27, and 101. But, since the Psalms and Proverbs are peppered with these truths, the Valiant must also be peppered with them. When the world tugs at you from all directions, it may take courage to fear the Lord and keep His commandments. But it is wise to do so. Understand?

YOUR THOUGHTS

_____

_____

_____

_____

_____

_____

_____

_____

_____

TAKE AWAY

What have you learned or re-thought that will enhance your
walk with the Lord today?

_____

_____

_____

PRAY

_____

_____

_____

OBEY

All day. You can do it because He will do it through you if you
let Him.

DAY 106: Don't Be a Slow-Learner

Who is the man that fears the Lord? He shall teach him in the way He chooses.

Psalm 25:12

OBSERVE

Check the traits this scripture invokes:

Courage? _____   Boldness? _____   Honor? _____

Steadfastness? _____   Other? _____

MY THOUGHTS

Once you become a Christian, you are immediately enrolled in God's school. He is your teacher and your tutor. He teaches each Christian individually. Some students are attentive and learn quickly; others are truant and require much homework. But be assured that each individual lesson-plan is tailor-made from the Lord, and the goal is the same for everyone: *fear God and keep His commandments.* (Ecclesiastes 12:13).

YOUR THOUGHTS

_____

_____

_____

_____

_____

_____

_____

_____

_____

TAKE AWAY

What have you learned or re-thought that will enhance your
walk with the Lord today?

_____

_____

_____

PRAY

_____

_____

_____

OBEY

All day. You can do it because He will do it through you if you
let Him.

DAY 107: Keep Reading

For the commandment is a lamp, and the law is a light.
Proverbs 6:23(a)

OBSERVE

Check the traits this scripture invokes:

Courage? _____   Boldness? _____   Honor? _____

Steadfastness? _____   Other? _____

MY THOUGHTS

As Christians, we have no reason to stumble around in spiritual darkness. With the Bible as our Guidebook and the Holy Spirit as our Guide, our spiritual pathway will be well-lighted. But spiritual light does not come by wishful thinking. We must read the Guidebook and let the Guide, guide. Every day.

YOUR THOUGHTS

_____

_____

_____

_____

_____

_____

_____

_____

_____

TAKE AWAY

What have you learned or re-thought that will enhance your walk with the Lord today?

_____

_____

_____

PRAY

_____

_____

_____

OBEY

All day. You can do it because He will do it through you if you let Him.

DAY 108: Stubbornness Is Not a Virtue

So, I gave them over to their own stubborn heart, to walk in their own counsels.
Psalm 81:12

OBSERVE

Check the traits this scripture invokes:

Courage? _____   Boldness? _____   Honor? _____

Steadfastness? _____   Other? _____

MY THOUGHTS

Never confuse stubbornness with determination. Determination is perseverance in reaching a worthy, God-given goal, never giving up, believing God. Stubbornness is self-will, "having my way, no matter what God or anyone else says." According to *I Samuel 15:23, stubbornness is as iniquity or idolatry.* Stubbornness may get you your way, but is it worth the cost? It cost King Saul his throne.

YOUR THOUGHTS

_____

_____

_____

_____

_____

_____

_____

_____

_____

TAKE AWAY

What have you learned or re-thought that will enhance your walk with the Lord today?

_____

_____

_____

PRAY

_____

_____

_____

OBEY

All day. You can do it because He will do it through you if you let Him.

DAY 109: Praise the Lord!

Praise the Lord! I will praise God with my whole heart.
Psalm 111:1a

OBSERVE

Check the traits this scripture invokes:

Courage? _____   Boldness? _____   Honor? _____

Steadfastness? _____   Other? _____

MY THOUGHTS

Don't let "Praise the Lord" become just a churchy cliché in your conversation. Don't let those words become a mere catchphrase instead of grateful praise. When you say, "Praise the Lord," praise the Lord. With your whole heart.

YOUR THOUGHTS

_____

_____

_____

_____

_____

_____

_____

_____

TAKE AWAY

What have you learned or re-thought that will enhance your walk with the Lord today?

_____

_____

_____

PRAY

_____

_____

_____

OBEY

All day. You can do it because He will do it through you if you let Him.

DAY 110: Pure Delight

*Delight yourself also in the Lord, and He shall
give you the desires of your heart.*
Psalms 37:4

OBSERVE

Check the traits this scripture invokes:

Courage? _____   Boldness? _____   Honor? _____

Steadfastness? _____   Other? _____

MY THOUGHTS

Even in troubling times, if you sincerely thank God for your salvation, for your eternal security, and for the indwelling of the Holy Spirit who empowers and directs you, you will have a change of countenance and a change of attitude. Maybe even a change of desire. That is delight. When the desire of your heart is in line with God's desire for your heart, He will give you that desire. That is pure delight.

YOUR THOUGHTS

_____

_____

_____

_____

_____

_____

_____

_____

_____

TAKE AWAY

What have you learned or re-thought that will enhance your walk with the Lord today?

_____

_____

_____

PRAY

_____

_____

_____

OBEY

All day. You can do it because He will do it through you if you let Him.

DAY 111: I'm Forgiven

I said, "I will confess my transgressions to the Lord,"
and You forgave the iniquity of my sin.
Psalm 32:5b

OBSERVE
Check the traits this scripture invokes:

Courage? _____   Boldness? _____   Honor? _____

Steadfastness? _____   Other? _____

MY THOUGHTS
Your after-salvation sins will not get you unsaved, but they will give you a guilty conscience and perhaps shame or disgrace. Confess and repent, and God will forgive you. Satan may keep reminding you of your transgressions, and when he does, remind him that *As far as the east is from the west, so far has He removed our transgressions from us (Psalm 103:12)*. So, get behind me, Satan.

YOUR THOUGHTS

_____

_____

_____

_____

_____

_____

_____

_____

_____

TAKE AWAY.

What have you learned or re-thought that will enhance your walk with the Lord today?

_____

_____

_____

PRAY

_____

_____

_____

OBEY

All day. You can do it because He will do it through you if you let Him.

DAY 112: Have You Ever Wondered...?

The Lord is on my side; I will not fear.
Psalm 118:6(a)

OBSERVE

Check the traits this scripture invokes:

Courage? _____   Boldness? _____   Honor? _____

Steadfastness? _____   Other? _____

MY THOUGHTS

When two Christians are praying opposing prayers, whose side is the Lord on? In the Garden of Gethsemane, Jesus prayed, *"Father, if it is Your will, take this cup away from Me; nevertheless, not My will, but yours be done" (Luke 22:42)*. Was God on His side? Was His prayer answered? Did He fear? Today's scripture verse, along with Jesus' prayer should give you an answer and maybe even change the way you pray. What do you think?

YOUR THOUGHTS

_____

_____

_____

_____

_____

_____

_____

_____

_____

TAKE AWAY

What have you learned or re-thought that will enhance your walk with the Lord today?

_____

_____

_____

PRAY

_____

_____

_____

OBEY

All day. You can do it because He will do it through you if you let Him.

DAY 113: What is Happening?

Look among the nations and watch – be utterly astounded!
For I will work a work in your days which you would not believe,
though it were told to you.
Habakkuk 1:5

OBSERVE

Check the traits this scripture invokes:

Courage? ____   Boldness? ____   Honor? ____

Steadfastness? ____   Other? _____

MY THOUGHTS

God warned Judah to repent of their sins, but they did not. After all, they were God's chosen people living in the City of God. What could go wrong? Everything. Jerusalem was destroyed, and the people were taken captive to Babylon. God's warning today is the same to us as it was to Judah: repent and return to God. Individually and as a nation. Or be utterly astounded.

YOUR THOUGHTS

_____

_____

_____

_____

_____

_____

_____

_____

_____

TAKE AWAY

What have you learned or re-thought that will enhance your walk with the Lord today?

_____

_____

_____

PRAY

_____

_____

_____

OBEY

All day. You can do it because He will do it through you if you let Him.

DAY 114: You Are Not Your Own

*Or do you not know that your body is the
temple of the Holy Spirit who is in you,
whom you have from God, and you are not your own.
For you were bought at a price; therefore, glorify God
in your body and in your spirit, which are God's.*
I Corinthians 6:19-20

OBSERVE

Check the traits this scripture invokes:

Courage? ____   Boldness? ____   Honor? ____

Steadfastness? ____   Other? _____

MY THOUGHTS

When you became a Christian, your body became the temple, the dwelling place, of the Holy Spirit. Your body, as well as your spirit, is to bring glory to God. Therefore, abuse of the body, whether by gluttony, addiction, physical neglect, immodesty, sexual immorality, or any other abuse is damage to someone else' property: God's.

YOUR THOUGHTS

_____

_____

_____

_____

_____

_____

_____

_____

_____

TAKE AWAY

What have you learned or re-thought that will enhance your walk with the Lord today?

_____

_____

_____

PRAY

_____

_____

_____

OBEY

All day. You can do it because He will do it through you if you let Him.

DAY 115: What Says the Lord of Hosts?

"[…] Thus says the Lord of hosts, 'Return to Me,' says the Lord of hosts, 'and I will return to you,' says the Lord of hosts."
Zechariah 1:3

OBSERVE

Check the traits this scripture invokes:

Courage? _____   Boldness? _____   Honor? _____

Steadfastness? _____   Other? _____

MY THOUGHTS

If you are feeling that the Lord is far away, not hearing your prayers, and maybe even feeling like He is angry with you, what *says the Lord of hosts? "Return to Me, and I will return to you."* And how do you return? You repent and obey. So, to make this verse in plain language, we might say, "Thus says the Lord of hosts, 'Repent and obey,' says the Lord of hosts, 'and I will return to you,' says the Lord of hosts." What say you?

YOUR THOUGHTS

_____

_____

_____

_____

_____

_____

_____

_____

_____

TAKE AWAY

What have you learned or re-thought that will enhance your walk with the Lord today?

_____

_____

_____

PRAY

_____

_____

_____

OBEY

All day. You can do it because He will do it through you if you let Him.

DAY 116: Till Your Land

He who tills his land will have plenty of bread,
but he who follows frivolity will have poverty enough.
Proverbs 28:19

OBSERVE

Check the traits this scripture invokes:

Courage? _____   Boldness? _____   Honor? _____

Steadfastness? _____   Other? _____

MY THOUGHTS

If you have a job, do it to the best of your ability; if you do not have a job, find one; if you cannot find a job, use your skills, your talents, your God-given abilities in whatever ways God directs you. Laziness and frivolous living bring poverty. That is a poor way to live.

YOUR THOUGHTS

_____

_____

_____

_____

_____

_____

_____

_____

_____

TAKE AWAY

What have you learned or re-thought that will enhance your walk with the Lord today?

_____

_____

_____

PRAY

_____

_____

_____

OBEY

All day. You can do it because He will do it through you if you let Him.

DAY 117: Be Prospered

He who is of a proud heart stirs up strife,
but he who trusts in the Lord will be prospered.
Proverbs 28:25

OBSERVE

Check the traits this scripture invokes:

Courage? _____   Boldness? _____   Honor? _____

Steadfastness? _____   Other? _____

MY THOUGHTS

Prosperity comes in many forms, including wealth, health, physical delight, knowledge, and spiritual wisdom, to name a few. Trust the Lord to prosper you in His way as you are obedient to Him. Do not let a proud or greedy heart put up a barrier so that you miss out on whatever prosperity God has for you. That stirs up strife in your life.

YOUR THOUGHTS

_____

_____

_____

_____

_____

_____

_____

_____

_____

TAKE AWAY

What have you learned or re-thought that will enhance your walk with the Lord today?

_____

_____

_____

PRAY

_____

_____

_____

OBEY

All day. You can do it because He will do it through you if you let Him.

DAY 118: Keep Short Accounts

Owe no one anything except to love one another,
for he who loves another has fulfilled the law.

Romans 13:8

OBSERVE

Check the traits this scripture invokes:

Courage? _____   Boldness? _____   Honor? _____

Steadfastness? _____   Other? _____

MY THOUGHTS

Pay your debts: monetarily, physically, verbally, spiritually. Write that overdue letter. Return the tool you borrowed. Apologize for unkindness. If you have strayed from the Lord, repent. Keep your debts paid and your sins confessed. But do it all in love as Christ commanded (John 13:34) and as Paul commended (I Corinthians 13). Otherwise. there is still a balance due, because love is the fulfillment of the law.

YOUR THOUGHTS

_____

_____

_____

_____

_____

_____

_____

_____

_____

TAKE AWAY

What have you learned or re-thought that will enhance your
walk with the Lord today?

_____

_____

_____

PRAY

_____

_____

_____

OBEY

All day. You can do it because He will do it through you if you
let Him.

DAY 119: Scripture Search

For whatever things were written before
were written for our learning,
that we, through the patience and comfort
of the scriptures, might have hope.
Romans 15:4

OBSERVE

Check the traits this scripture invokes:

Courage? _____   Boldness? _____   Honor? _____

Steadfastness? _____   Other? _____

MY THOUGHTS

When things seem hopeless, what should we do? Search the scriptures. Before things seem hopeless, what should we do? Search the scriptures. When life seems full of hope, what should we do. Search the scriptures. That is why they were written: for our learning and patience and comfort, to give us hope. But we must do the homework.

YOUR THOUGHTS

_____

_____

_____

_____

_____

_____

_____

_____

_____

TAKE AWAY

What have you learned or re-thought that will enhance your walk with the Lord today?

_____

_____

_____

PRAY

_____

_____

_____

OBEY

All day. You can do it because He will do it through you if you let Him.

DAY 120: Who Are Your Heroes?

So now we call the proud blessed, for those
who do wickedness are raised up;
They even tempt God and go free.
Malachi 3:15

OBSERVE

Check the traits this scripture invokes:

Courage? _____   Boldness? _____   Honor? _____

Steadfastness? _____   Other? _____

MY THOUGHTS

Be careful that you do not allow an ungodly culture to capture and transform your hopes and dreams and make ungodly people your heroes. That is what Israel did. They turned from God with their hearts while professing Him with their lips. But they eventually paid the price by being conquered and enslaved. Make sure that your lips and heart are on the same wavelength.

YOUR THOUGHTS

_____

_____

_____

_____

_____

_____

_____

_____

_____

TAKE AWAY

What have you learned or re-thought that will enhance your walk with the Lord today?

_____

_____

_____

PRAY

_____

_____

_____

OBEY

All day. You can do it because He will do it through you if you let Him.

DAY 121: The Morning News

Through the Lord's mercies we are not consumed,
because His compassions fail not; they are new
every morning; great is Your faithfulness.
Lamentations 3:22-23

OBSERVE

Check the traits this scripture invokes:

Courage? _____   Boldness? _____   Honor? _____

Steadfastness? _____   Other? _____

MY THOUGHTS

If you are not being renewed in your spirit and in your mind and in
your walk with the Lord every morning, then you are missing out
on His mercies and compassion. They are NEW every morning.
Not yesterday's blessings. Today's. They are yours for the claiming,
no matter what your situation may be. Ask the Holy Spirit to fill
your soul and renew your mind. And then, have a good morning.

YOUR THOUGHTS

_____

_____

_____

_____

_____

_____

_____

_____

_____

TAKE AWAY

What have you learned or re-thought that will enhance your walk with the Lord today?

_____

_____

_____

PRAY

_____

_____

_____

OBEY

All day. You can do it because He will do it through you if you let Him.

DAY 122: Whose Standards?

Honor the Lord with your possessions and with the firstfruits of all your increase; so your barns will be filled with plenty, and your vats will overflow with new wine.

Proverbs 3:9-10

OBSERVE

Check the traits this scripture invokes:

Courage? _____   Boldness? _____   Honor? _____

Steadfastness? _____   Other? _____

MY THOUGHTS

This verse is not just about giving, it is about honoring the Lord with everything you possess. Possessing and giving are spiritual issues; possessing and not giving are definitely spiritual issues. If your larder is not full and your vats are not overflowing, check your standards of living and giving. Are they the world's standards or God's?

YOUR THOUGHTS

_____

_____

_____

_____

_____

_____

_____

_____

_____

TAKE AWAY

What have you learned or re-thought that will enhance your walk with the Lord?

_____

_____

_____

PRAY

_____

_____

_____

OBEY

All day. You can do it because He will do it through you if you let Him.

DAY 123: Conclusion: We Are More Than Conquerors

Who shall separate us from the love of Christ?
Shall tribulation, or distress, or persecution,
or famine, or nakedness, or peril,
or sword? ... Yet, in all these things, we are more than conquerors
through Him who loved us. For I am persuaded that neither death
nor life, nor angels nor principalities nor powers, nor things present
nor things to come, nor height nor depth, nor any other created
thing shall be able to separate us from the love of God which is in
Jesus Christ our Lord.
Romans 8:35; 37-39

OBSERVE

Check the traits this scripture invokes:

Courage? _____   Boldness? _____   Honor? _____

Steadfastness? _____   Other? _____

MY THOUGHTS

Tribulation, distress, persecution, famine, nakedness, peril, the sword: I do not know of any hardship or tragedy that is not covered by these words. The Bible does not promise that Christians will have none of these tragedies. But it does promise that no matter what the hardship may be, God will see us through it. He will not only see us through it, but He will also see us through it victoriously. And not only victoriously, but super-victoriously. More than conquerors! More than conquerors through Him who loved us.

Now, these words are easy to say to someone else who is going through a life conflict. But what about when you or I are going through the most difficult, the saddest point in our lives? What about when tragedies that make no sense occur? What about the times when we can quote the words of scripture but do not feel the comfort of them? It is through such times as these that the scriptures must come ALIVE for us. They must become not just words on a page but LIVING WORDS in our hearts. And how does that happen? Through God's grace and our faith. We must use the same faith that saved us to fill us with the powerful truth that NOTHING can separate us from the love of God. NOTHING. Not life nor death nor angels nor principalities nor powers nor things present nor things to come nor height nor depth nor any other created thing – NOTHING can separate us from the love of God which is in Christ Jesus our Lord.

Those are powerful, life-changing, life-giving words. They are victorious words. And it is by believing and having faith that these words are true that **The Valiant** become more than conquerors.

YOUR THOUGHTS

_____

_____

_____

_____

_____

_____

_____

_____

_____

TAKE AWAY

What have you learned or re-thought that will enhance your walk with the Lord today?

_____

_____

_____

_____

_____

_____

PRAY

_____

_____

_____

OBEY

All day. You can do it because He will do it through you if you let Him.

SCRIPTURE REFERENCES IN ALPHABETICAL ORDER

Scripture	Day	Scripture	Day
Acts		**Hebrews**	
2:21	17	13:5b	33
I Corinthians		**Isaiah**	
6:19,20	114	6:8c	71
13:3	73	26:3	37
II Corinthians		**James**	
4:2(a)	28	1:5	27
9:7	39	1:17	77
Deuteronomy		**Jeremiah**	
7:18	33	29:11	82
29:29	53	**Job**	
Ecclesiastes		28:28	10
2:24	14	32:9	10
12:13	18;106	**John**	
Galatians		7:38	16
3:11b	10	8:12	8
		10:10	57
Habakkuk		14:6	88
1:5	113	14:27	37
2:4b	10	16:33	13
3:17-19	81	17:15	103
		20:31	15

Scripture	Day	Scripture	Day
I John		**Matthew**	
1:9	84	6:33a	22;95
3:23,24a	85	11:28-30	63
		25:40	38
III John			
1:2	87	**Micah**	
1:4	88	4:5	94
		6:8	70
Joshua			
1:9	35;54	**I Peter**	
24: 15a	64	1:3	43
24:15c	65	1:4,5	57
		1:15,16	70
Jude		1:25	68
1:12b	93	2:1-3	72
1:24	96	2:4,5a	75
		2:5	76
Judges			
21:25	80	**II Peter**	
		1:3	79
Lamentations			
3:22-23	121	**Philippians**	
		4:13	99
Luke			
6:45b	55	**Proverbs**	
22:42	112	3:5,6	34
24:45	4	3:9-10	122
		4:23	55
Malachi		6:23a	107
3:15	120	9:10	27;101
		11:2	61
		11:25	25

Scripture	Day	Scripture	Day
Proverbs		**Psalm**	
12:18	26	25:12	106
13:19	32	27:1b	20
13:20	27	31:14b	58
15:8	67	31:15a	58
16:3	100	31:24	59
16:16	101	32:5b	111
16:20	99	33:12a	21
19:17	73	34:4	98
19:21	36	34:12-14	95
20:7	77	37:1a;7b;8b	22
21:4	78	37:4	110
21:13	39	42:5a,11a	23
21:24	78	43:5a	23
21:25,26	40	45:4a	62
23:4	41	46:1-3	91
23:17a	6	50:23	24
24:5	44	51:6	60
25:26	46	55:22	31
25:28	9	60:12	1
27:2	61	71:9,18	29
28:19	116	73:26	66
28:25	117	78:6a,7,8a	69
30:5	52	78:72	42
		81:10	102
Psalm		81:12	108
5:3	83	86:11	2
11:3	86	100:5	74
12:5	89	101:2b	3
18:29	30	101:5b	78
19:14	56	103:12	111
23:3a;4c	19	106:15	5

Scripture	Day		Scripture	Day
Psalm			**I Samuel**	
111:1a	109		12:24	90
111:10a	105		15:23	108
118:6a	112		15:24	92
119:133	7		16:1	97
119:147	45			
138:3	47		**I Thessalonians**	
138:3	48		4:10c,11,12b	104
139:13,14	11			
139:17,18a	82		**I Timothy**	
141:3,4	12		6:10	41
143:8a	49			
143:8b	50		**II Timothy**	
145:4	51		1:7	1
			1:7	33
Romans				
1:17b	10		**Zechariah**	
8:35,37-39	123		1:3	115
8:37	30			
13:8	118			
15:4	119			

ABOUT THE AUTHOR

Roy G. Miller is a retired International Mission Board (IMB) missionary. A graduate of Denver Seminary, Roy served on the staff at Applewood Baptist as church counselor and as church administrator. He and his wife, Janet, went on to serve for ten years in France, where they planted and pastored the International Baptist Church of Nice and the International Baptist Church of St. Paul de Vence. After retiring from the IMB, he joined the staff of First Baptist Church of Longview, Texas, as Minister of Missions. Once again, Roy attempted to retire, but his love of adventure and of working with international missions led him to Sofia, Bulgaria, where he became the interim pastor of International Baptist Church of Sofia. As an author, Roy G. Miller has contributed devotional material to Open Windows and to a devotional book, "The Chosen Path." Roy began writing The Valiant at age 86, an example that Bible study is a lifelong discipline. The Valiant is a culmination of his 75-plus years of studying God's word, preaching, teaching, and counseling others. A widower, Roy lives with his daughter, Michelle and his son-in-law, Jon Shearer, in Tampa, Florida.

www.ingramcontent.com/pod-product-compliance
Lightning Source LLC
Chambersburg PA
CBHW021716120626
46545CB00004B/1582